Daily Mail

THE
WORLD'S
smallest
HARDEST
CROSSWORDS

D1364556

hamlyn

An Hachette UK Company
www.hachette.co.uk

First published in Great Britain in 2010 by
Hamlyn, a division of Octopus Publishing Group Ltd
Endeavour House, 189 Shaftesbury Avenue
London WC2H 8JY
www.octopusbooks.co.uk

First published in this format in 2010

Copyright © Associated Newspapers Ltd / Knight Features Ltd 2010
Design copyright © Octopus Publishing Group Ltd 2010

The Daily Mail name and logo are registered trade marks of Associated
Newspapers Limited

All rights reserved. No part of this work may be reproduced or utilised in any
form or by any means, electronic or mechanical, including photocopying,
recording or by any information storage and retrieval system, without the
prior written permission of the publisher.

ISBN 978-0-600-62112-6

A CIP catalogue record for this book is available from the British Library

Printed and bound in the UK

10 9 8 7 6 5 4 3 2 1

Produced for Hamlyn by Knight Features Limited
20 Crescent Grove
London SW4 7AH
www.knightfeatures.co.uk

PUZZLES

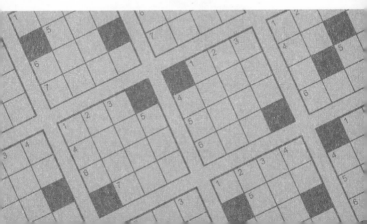

1

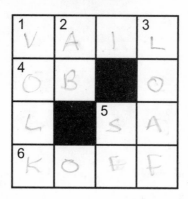

V	A	I	L
O	B	■	O
L	■	S	A
K	O	E	F

Across
1 Lower Sail; doff hat (4)
4 (L) died (abbr) (2)
5 (L) Without date (abbr) (2)
6 Small Dutch sailing boat (4)

Down
1 The Afrikaner people (4)
2 One of four blood types (2)
3 A cabbage-head (4)
5 (Mus) with sudden
emphasis (abbr) (2)

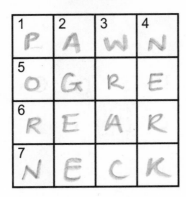

P	A	W	N
O	G	R	E
R	E	A	R
N	E	C	K

Across

1 Gallery, covered walk (4)
5 Stern person inspiring fear (4)
6 Hinder (4)
7 Impudence (4)

Down

1 'Blue' material (4)
2 (Scot) off the straight (4)
3 Successors to the ATS (4)
4 An irritating fool (4)

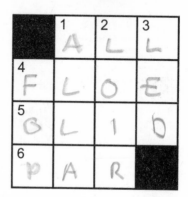

3

Across
1 ___ in ___; everything considered (3)
4 Floating ice field (4)
5 Smelling rank (4)
6 Without premium or discount (3)

Down
1 In the style of (It) (4)
2 Large European dormouse (4)
3 ___ captain; obsequious attendant (3)
4 Affected dandy (3)

4

Across
1 Port in the bay of Haifa (4)
5 The nictitating membrane (3)
6 A persistent scold (3)
7 Bout of excessive indulgence (4)

Down
2 Do odd jobs for work (4)
3 Rough hard stone (4)
4 Win or place (abbr) (2)
6 Not any (2)

5

S	E	A	
I	P	S	O
C	H	I	D
	A	S	E

Across
1 Seemingly limitless mass (3)
4 ___ facto: thereby (4)
6 Tackle aggressively (4)
7 Suffix denoting an enzyme (-3)

Down
1 (L) so, thus (3)
2 Hebrew dry goods measure (4)
3 Unaltered (2,2)
5 A joke; a drink (3)

Across
1 Drinking-mug (3)
4 Conceal, cover (4)
5 (Logic) therefore (4)
6 Fallow (3)

Down
1 Cover with wax (4)
2 Seaweed (4)
3 Artificial language (3)
4 Goddess of the dead,
   Loki's daughter (3)

7

Across
1 A 'business manager' (4)
4 Manx race (abbr) (1,1)
5 (Scot) a beloved (2)
6 (Mus) a middle part (4)

Down
1 Unfermented grape juice (4)
2 Doh (2)
3 The market-place (4)
5 ___ wohl (Ger): yes indeed (2)

8

F		S	
E		L	
T	R	I	P
A	N	T	S

Across

1 (Heraldry) horizontal band (4)
5 (Shakesp) prob. evil (4)
6 Small flock of sheep (4)
7 Social insects (4)

Down

1 Goat's, ewe's milk cheese (4)
2 Bring to someone (4)
3 Long cut (4)
4 Skink (4)

Across

1 (Shakesp) fuddled, drunk (3)
4 Squander (4)
5 Woman turned to for advice (4)
6 (Curling) mark aimed at (3)

Down

1 Soft down (4)
2 Old French fabric measure (4)
3 The sulks (3)
4 Lingo (3)

10

Across
1 Sickly-sweet (4)
5 Shepherd's pipe (3)
6 A newt (3)
7 Member of Mongoloid Chinese people (4)

Down
2 Bludgeon (4)
3 Green NZ parrot (4)
4 That (abbr) (2)
6 A Norse god (2)

Across

1 Gap between two conductors (3)
4 (Austr) wax-like edible larval secretion (4)
6 (Tasmania) mountain range (4)
7 Part of beef carcase (3)

Down

1 (Mus) high tone (3)
2 Plural of real (4)
3 (Grain) soften by soaking (4)
5 Show impertinent curiosity (3)

Across
1 Corporal, for one (abbr) (1,1,1)
4 A catfish (4)
5 Mine passage (4)
6 However (3)

Down
1 Point of intersection (4)
2 (Austr) backside (4)
3 Frequently (3)
4 Advance in life (3)

13

Across
1 In a frenzy (4)
4 Hundredth of a dong (2)
5 Alaska (abbr) (2)
6 (E Africa) short sword (4)

Down
1 Main stem or root (4)
2 __-meson, a subatomic particle (2)
3 Chinese date-plum (4)
5 Hail Mary (abbr) (1,1)

14

1	2	3	4
5			
6			
7			

Across

1 Attest legally and date (4)
5 Latin, wife (4)
6 Convex, semicircular moulding (4)
7 Solve problem, riddle (4)

Down

1 Poisonous NZ shrub (4)
2 Segment of gene consisting of codons (4)
3 A flock of mallards (4)
4 2nd Section of scherzo (4)

15

Across
1 Charged particle (3)
4 Tatar heavy wagon (4)
5 A hired thug (4)
6 Being, existence (3)

Down
1 A stirrup (4)
2 Oil, bulk ore vessels (4)
3 Indian slightly leavened bread (3)
4 A generation (3)

16

Across
1 Hindu divine snake (4)
5 Hawthorn flower (3)
6 A Low churchman (3)
7 African antelope (4)

Down
2 Muslim prince's title (4)
3 Sensational (4)
4 Ah, oh, alas (2)
6 Thereupon (2)

17

Across
1 Area between two anticyclones (3)
4 Greedy (4)
6 Transvestite panto character (4)
7 Cricket dismissal (1,1,1)

Down
1 No gentleman (3)
2 Cricket ground (4)
3 Mischievous child (4)
5 Early freshness (3)

18

Across
1 Vegas, Palmas (3)
4 Elude, cheat (4)
5 Very black (4)
6 Japanese drama (3)

Down
1 Floor covering (abbr) (4)
2 Ansate cross (4)
3 Hang above the line of sight (3)
4 ___ Shin Do, a form of acupressure (3)

Across
1 The service tree (4)
4 Media format (abbr) (1,1)
5 (Prefix) two (2-)
6 String toy (2-2)

Down
1 Practice crystal-gazing (4)
2 Reichenbach force (2)
3 Vivacity, spirit (4)
5 In reserve (2)

¹	²	³	⁴
⁵			
⁶			
⁷			

Across

1 Timber frame upright (4)
5 The Buckeye State (4)
6 A puddle, a plump (4)
7 Ways of escape (4)

Down

1 Indifferent (2-2)
2 You (4)
3 Island of the Outer Hebrides (4)
4 Sleep (4)

Across

1 Season of blackcock display (3)
4 Deep shade of light blue (4)
5 Bad of its kind (4)
6 Film section action replay facility (3)

Down

1 Country bordering Cambodia (4)
2 Public showing (4)
3 Low Island (3)
4 Indian title of respect (3)

22

Across

1 Nuts, acorns (4)
5 (Prefix) life (3)
6 Mushrooms of the Boletus genus (3)
7 Smart know-it-all (4)

Down

2 First victim of fratricide (4)
3 Slit in tread of tyre (4)
4 Shut (2)
6 (L)(abbr) about (2)

23

Across
1 ___ bonne heure: well done! (1,2)
4 Type of blue, green (4)
6 Dog's-tooth grass (4)
7 Sharp point of anything (3)

Down
1 Even if (3)
2 Conspicuous, sought-after person (4)
3 Maguey: American___ (4)
5 Sink (3)

Across

1 Fly maggot-parasitic in horses (3)
4 Western US liliaceous plant (4)
5 Bog fuel (4)
6 Prepare bomb to explode (3)

Down

1 Porter (4)
2 Ancient alphabet (4)
3 Something retrieved from rubbish (3)
4 Pool of aerated water (3)

25

Across
1 S-curved (4)
4 Fine jade (2)
5 (Prefix) primitive (2-)
6 An incarnation of Vishnu (4)

Down
1 An assize (4)
2 Old Shetland viol (2)
3 OT book (4)
5 Hesitant interjection (2)

1	2	3	4
5			
6			
7			

Across
1 Young salmon (4)
5 The sapi-utan (4)
6 To tirl (4)
7 (US) Diagram, plan (4)

Down
1 Sound car horn (4)
2 Indigo (4)
3 Sub____: privately (4)
4 Entranced (4)

27

Across

1 Vineyard; vintage (3)
4 Fish of cod family (4)
5 Except that mentioned (4)
6 (Horse) move to the right (3)

Down

1 Plant of cabbage family (4)
2 Stratagem (4)
3 Pick-up truck (3)
4 Drink measure (3)

28

Across
1 Outmoded doctrine (4)
5 Card game (3)
6 Always (1'2)
7 State of obligation (4)

Down
2 On the sheltered side (4)
3 A Wend (4)
4 An instant (2)
6 Leading journalist (abbr) (2)

29

Across
1 TV receiver (3)
4 Sixth of a drachma (4)
6 Apple (4)
7 Type of cat, rabbit (3)

Down
1 A concession (3)
2 (abbr) York (4)
3 Large book (4)
5 (L) law (3)

30

Across
1 Fruit syrup (3)
4 (Prefix) air (4-)
5 US college president (4)
6 Sheep in its 2nd year (3)

Down
1 ____-supper: a late meal (4)
2 The Beaver State (abbr) (4)
3 Name points of compass (3)
4 Ready, prone (3)

Across

1 Lubber, clumsy fellow (4)
4 Male (2)
5 (Abbr) those not holding commissions (1,1)
6 Steal cattle (4)

Down

1 Herring-related fish (4)
2 Royal pronoun (2)
3 (US) to vomit (4)
5 Owing to (2)

Across
1 Roman garment (4)
5 Coarse seaside grass (4)
6 Anything very small (4)
7 ___-poly; round, podgy (4)

Down
1 Bulgarian King (4)
2 Damask rose oil (4)
3 Prison (4)
4 Host (4)

33

Across
1 (Scot) a fit of perversity (3)
4 Make sign of cross over (4)
5 Paint medium (4)
6 Miner's wedge (3)

Down
1 Goddess of Earth (4)
2 Not bearing young, not yielding milk (4)
3 Being, existence (3)
4 To soak (3)

Across
1 White paint for the face (4)
5 Shakespeare interjection of boisterous emotion (3)
6 Inmate of gulag (3)
7 Portent (4)

Down
2 Sound to clear the throat (4)
3 Vapour steam (4)
4 Be just good enough (2)
6 Hybrid of yak, cow (2)

35

Across
1 (Prefix) double (3-)
4 Stop (4)
6 Honey-buzzard (4)
7 A brew (3)

Down
1 (Welsh) dim-witted (3)
2 Make keen (4)
3 Time long past (4)
5 Collection of anecdotes (3)

36

Across
1 St Anthony's cross (3)
4 Pulley with ropes not parallel (4)
5 Friends, acquaintances (4)
6 Telecom union (abbr) (1,1,1)

Down
1 Taunt, upbraid (4)
2 Polynesian demigod (4)
3 Exclamation of repugnance (3)
4 Travel on snow (3)

37

1	2		3
4		■	
	■	5	
6			

Across
1 Heroin (4)
4 (Scot) a jackdaw (2)
5 Constituted by (2)
6 Depression in bottom of glass container (4)

Down
1 Not to read all (4)
2 (L) about (abbr) (2)
3 A talent (4)
5 In progress (2)

Across
1 ___fan Tutte, Mozart opera (4)
5 Wooden coffers (4)
6 Unhappy (4)
7 Unfledged hawk (4)

Down
1 Goal, as in ice hockey (4)
2 Paris air terminal (4)
3 Predatory gull-like bird (4)
4 Distinctive doctrines (4)

39

Across
1 (Scot) cows (3)
4 Catch holding gun at cock (4)
5 ___ -errand (Scot): for the express purpose (4)
6 (Slang) a laugh (3)

Down
1 Gambling game similar to bingo (4)
2 Idle or stupid talk (4)
3 Before (3)
4 Old woollen cloth (3)

40

Across

1 Hawk's short leg-strap (4)
5 Sea bream (3)
6 Hoax, false tale (3)
7 Chinese monetary unit (4)

Down

2 Hunter son of Isaac (4)
3 Japanese title of exalted person (4)
4 Steradian (abbr) (2)
6 Multiplied into (2)

Across

1 Bag-like structure (3)
4 The E of QEF (4)
6 Pheasant's nest, brood (4)
7 Early freshness (3)

Down

1 One hundredth of a rupiah (3)
2 Barren (4)
3 Pet lamb (4)
5 To work up, taw (3)

Across
1 Public house (3)
4 Indulge in lovemaking (4)
5 Black-and-white toothed whale (4)
6 Albanian currency unit (3)

Down
1 (L) concerning (2,2)
2 Fit arrow to bowstring (4)
3 A former print union (abbr) (1,1,1)
4 Old French coin (3)

43

Across

1 Where the high table stands (4)
4 (L) in the same place (abbr) (2)
5 Modern scientific system of units (abbr) (1,1)
6 (US) magic spell, charm (4)

Down

1 Carpe___ ; enjoy the present (4)
2 Rank above OS (abbr) (1,1)
3 (Orkney, Shetland) a hut (4)
5 Jesuits (abbr) (1,1)

44

1	2	3	4
5			
6			
7			

Across
1 A northern European (4)
5 Inter____: among other things (4)
6 A false god (4)
7 To lash out with (4)

Down
1 One's pet project (4)
2 Winglike bone processes (4)
3 Ananias (4)
4 Converse (4)

Across

1 Dolce____niente: pleasant idleness (3)
4 (L) goods (4)
5 Nautical hail (4)
6 Public house (3)

Down

1 Hot dry Alpine valley wind (4)
2 At another time (4)
3 A skate (3)
4 Bachelor of Engineering (abbr) (1,1,1)

Across

1 Ait (4)
5 Impose on, hoax (3)
6 Ethiopian cereal grass (3)
7 (Golf) strike ground with sole of club (4)

Down

2 African butter-nut tree (4)
3 Turn ship towards wind (4)
4 ___ rule; demarcates a parenthetical thought (2)
6 Consumption (abbr) (1,1)

Across
1 (L) force, power (3)
4 Flag; part of eye (4)
6 Type of shark (4)
7 Which was to be proved (abbr) (1,1,1)

Down
1 Energy, vigour (3)
2 Mesopotamia (4)
3 (Scot) rill, small ditch (4)
5 To poll, clip (3)

Across

1 The mouth (3)
4 Indian stringed instrument (4)
5 Threatening, disquieting (4)
6 'The Beggar's' Opera librettist (3)

Down

1 (Prefix) a thousand million (4-)
2 Not more (4)
3 Second tine of deer's horn (3)
4 Cornish crystal-lined rock cavity (3)

49

1	2		3
4		■	
	■	5	
6			

Across

1 Problematical (4)
4 Behold! (2)
5 Link of alternatives (2)
6 Mark of servitude (4)

Down

1 ___whacker (Austr) conman (4)
2 Soccer organisation (abbr) (1,1)
3 Ready, prepared, quick (4)
5 Endorsement (1,1)

50

¹	²	³	⁴
⁵			
⁶			
⁷			

Across
1 Make fast by a lashing (4)
5 Eddo (4)
6 Of a wing (4)
7 Mythical animal, horse with tusks (4)

Down
1 Rope bracing mast (4)
2 Rhythmic pattern in Indian music (4)
3 Spoken (4)
4 Opening of sweat gland (4)

Across

1 Trigonometrical function (3)
4 Synagogue (4)
5 In plentiful supply (4)
6 A wile, trick (3)

Down

1 (India) newly-formed island (4)
2 Eject (4)
3 Secretive (3)
4 Seemingly limitless mass (3)

52

Across
1 Three-handed, 32-card game (4)
5 Fuss (3)
6 Grape (3)
7 Catch engaging with ratchet (4)

Down
2 Plant of pepper family, narcotic drink (4)
3 (Spenser) daunt, subdue (4)
4 Along with (2)
6 Riding (2)

Across

1 Metric land measure (3)
4 (Pharm) (abbr) gallon (4)
6 A gallows (4)
7 Deuce (3)

Down

1 Perform (3)
2 (Austr) lively party (4)
3 (Falconry) plunge into water (4)
5 (Prefix) Earth (3-)

Across

1 Enemy (3)

4 Tale of adventure, romance (4)

5 Accompanied vocal solo (4)

6 ___-John: Scottish parish minister (3)

Down

1 Companion, mate (4)

2 (Suffix) diseased condition (-4)

3 Member of lowest Japanese class (3)

4 Female leg (3)

Across

1 Matweed (4)
4 (L)(abbr) died (2)
5 End of war v Germany, 1945 (abbr) (1,1)
6 Taste, relish (4)

Down

1 (Austr) a fool (4)
2 Rank above OS (abbr) (1,1)
3 An assembly, council (4)
5 Déjà ___ : old stuff (2)

56

Across
1 On the top (4)
5 Indian of gardener caste (4)
6 Face (4)
7 18th letter of Hebrew alphabet (4)

Down
1 Electrical measures (abbr) (4)
2 A S African weaver bird (4)
3 Rank-smelling (4)
4 Pox! Pest! (4)

57

Across
1 A cat (3)
4 Old Person (4)
5 Nipa palm (4)
6 Sleep phase (abbr) (1,1,1)

Down
1 Particle of dust (4)
2 Ancient alphabet (4)
3 Pain, torture (3)
4 (Animal) off (3)

Across
1 A W African gazelle (4)
5 100 stotinki (3)
6 Membranous outgrowth on fruit (3)
7 ___ -mecum, a pocket-companion (4)

Down
2 A jar, urn (4)
3 A mine tunnel (4)
4 A Bible version (abbr) (1,1)
6 A Bible version (abbr) (1,1)

59

Across

1 Central American crude rubber (3)
4 Build up (4)
6 Gratuity, bribe (4)
7 Artificial language, launched 1961 (3)

Down

1 Indian plant of bean family (3)
2 Be inclined (4)
3 Manoeuvre little by little (4)
5 Greek letter printed P (3)

60

Across
1 Vintage (3)
4 Type of squirrel fur (4)
5 (Austr) afternoon (4)
6 Member of N American Indian people (3)

Down
1 Carry around, with difficulty (4)
2 To split (4)
3 (Prefix) posterior part (3-)
4 The digamma (3)

61

1	**2**		**3**
4		■	
	■	**5**	
6			

Across
1 Pasture for one cow (4)
4 Batting (2)
5 Precise position in space or time (2)
6 Discount on foreign bill of exchange (4)

Down
1 Hindu god (4)
2 Acceptable (2)
3 ___ perpetuo: fast, non-stop music (4)
5 Small edible Japanese fish (2)

1	2	3	4
5			
6			
7			

Across
1 ___ trac: a form of backgammon (4)
5 Of an unspecified person or people (4)
6 Aqua ___: clean water (4)
7 Start play (4)

Down
1 A literal (abbr) (4)
2 (Scot) sale by public auction (4)
3 (L) by right, by law (4)
4 Measure of capacity for herrings (4)

Across
1 Hebrew liquid measure (3)
4 Denoting films (prefix) (4-)
5 To (4)
6 Image of oneself (3)

Down
1 Asafoetida (4)
2 To part of (math) (4)
3 (Prefix) revised in new form (3-)
4 Insert into a script (3)

64

Across
1 One's counterpart (abbr) (4)
5 A pollack (3)
6 Tiny amount of money (3)
7 Local Anglo-Saxon militia (4)

Down
2 Game manoeuvre (4)
3 Rain heavily (4)
4 (L) died (abbr) (2)
6 (Mus) with sudden emphasis (abbr) (2)

65

1	2	3	
4			5
6			
	7		

Across
1 To put off (3)
4 Salt Lake City state (4)
6 A challenge (4)
7 To drain (3)

Down
1 The buttocks (3)
2 Octave of a festival (4)
3 Unadorned (4)
5 Fell with blows (3)

	1	2	3
4			
5			
6			

Across
1 A drowned valley (3)
4 Instalment of a serial publication (4)
5 Golden-yellow id variety (4)
6 Turkish male address (3)

Down
1 ____-supper: a late meal (4)
2 Risky (4)
3 Took nourishment (3)
4 A gear-cutting tool (3)

1	2		3
4		■	
	■	5	
6			

Across
1 Not clerical (4)
4 A bone (2)
5 Electrical measure (abbr) (2)
6 Creamy fruit dessert (4)

Down
1 (Scot) palm of the hand (4)
2 For instance (2)
3 Chimney cover (4)
5 Stunning blow (abbr) (1,1)

1	2	3	4
5			
6			
7			

Across
1 Prates (4)
5 Hautboy (4)
6 Force producing acceleration (4)
7 Tie up animal (4)

Down
1 Theatre gallery (4)
2 Pay as a penalty (4)
3 (L) goods (4)
4 A sudden heeling (4)

Across
1 Knows (3)
4 A simpleton (4)
5 Independent African chieftain (4)
6 Obstruction (3)

Down
1 The belly (4)
2 Death anniversary (4)
3 Norse war-god (3)
4 Take shape (3)

1	2	3	4
■	5		
6			■
7			

Across

1 Horse mackerel (4)
5 Pounds, shillings and pence (abbr) (1,1,1)
6 Paste of fermented taro root (3)
7 Horse's canine tooth (4)

Down

2 A dominant idea (4)
3 Unattended (2,2)
4 Gave to God (L) (abbr) (1,1)
6 Fitness instructor (abbr) (1,1)

Across
1 Be still (3)
4 Exploits (4)
6 A W African monkey (4)
7 In point of fact (3)

Down
1 To beat (3)
2 One uncritically admired (4)
3 Liquid heating vessel (4)
5 Suppose as a hypothesis (3)

72

Across

1 Away (3)
4 Set of players at quadrille (4)
5 A young herring (4)
6 Amiss (3)

Down

1 Defeat, baffle (4)
2 An undulation (4)
3 Long practised (3)
4 23rd letter of Greek alphabet (3)

73

1	2		3
4		■	
	■	5	
6			

Across
1 ____ cloud, of frozen comet nuclei (4)
4 (Sound, special) effects (abbr) (1,1)
5 Has existence (2)
6 Yellowhammer (4)

Down
1 (US Black slang) a white person (4)
2 Bovine animal (2)
3 To card, comb (4)
5 Playground game (2)

Across

1 Spawn of shellfish (4)
5 Be silent (4)
6 Affection of superiority (4)
7 Exposed piece at backgammon (4)

Down

1 An attempt (4)
2 Bucket (4)
3 (Prefix) tip, point (4-)
4 Examine critically (4)

75

Across
1 FBI agent (3)
4 Jar, urn (4)
5 Barytes in platy crystals (4)
6 Pointed instrument (3)

Down
1 A gust of wind (4)
2 Jewish month (4)
3 Indian postal service (3)
4 S American wood-sorrel (3)

Across

1 Tatar screened wagon (4)
5 A vast age (3)
6 Sturdy (sheep disease) (3)
7 A big lie (4)

Down

2 To stop, check (4)
3 Portend (4)
4 If (2)
6 Failure to play (cribbage) (2)

Across
1 Whisper hoarsely (3)
4 Passed on by word of mouth (4)
6 Aniseed liqueur (4)
7 Metal plate on boot sole (3)

Down
1 Disapproving sound (3)
2 Aurochs (4)
3 Level building to the ground (4)
5 Computer record (3)

Across
1 Heated pool (3)
4 Shadow, shelter (4)
5 Dog-salmon (4)
6 Likely to (3)

Down
1 Straw beehive (4)
2 Hurl shot (4)
3 Turkish commander (3)
4 Jamaican reggae-like music (3)

Across

1 A narrow strait (4)
4 With reference to (2)
5 King Edward (abbr) (1,1)
6 Artificial rubber (4)

Down

1 (Mountaineering) steel link with spring clip (4)
2 You (2)
3 S American wild cat (4)
5 Half an em (2)

1	2	3	4
5			
6			
7			

Across

1 Chinese ounce (4)
5 Eye lecherously (4)
6 Yaws (4)
7 Yes (4)

Down

1 Punch's dog (4)
2 Shivering fit (4)
3 Island, chief town Portoferraio (4)
4 Sister of Rachel (4)

Across
1 Honey (3)
4 Carry on (4)
5 Symbol for a velar nasal consonant (4)
6 Cha (3)

Down
1 Sorcerer (4)
2 Costard's enigma (4)
3 Yarn measure (3)
4 A hare (3)

Across
1 This tooth, a molar (4)
5 Murmur softly (3)
6 A female (3)
7 Wood, matter (4)

Down
2 Painful (4)
3 Christmas carol (4)
4 Success (2)
6 Hush (2)

83

Across
1 Breakfast roll (3)
4 Individual (4)
6 Hyperbolic secant (4)
7 Freedom of action (3)

Down
1 (Computer) number of conductors forming circuit (3)
2 Freshly (4)
3 Magpie genus (4)
5 Your (3)

84

Across
1 ___ pro nobis: pray for us (3)
4 Grey (4)
5 Eat away (4)
6 Suffix denoting country of origin (-3)

Down
1 Table scraps (4)
2 Form potato into strands (4)
3 Volcanic dust (3)
4 A radio-navigation system (3)

85

Across
1 A minnow, samlet (4)
4 (Prefix) original (2-)
5 Takes place (2)
6 Unwilling (4)

Down
1 Go head over heels (4)
2 Income tax authority (abbr) (1,1)
3 Solid graphite floating on molten iron (4)
5 Personal magnetism (2)

1	2	3	4
5			
6			
7			

Across

1 Grapeskins, refuse from wine making (4)
5 Concert-halls (4)
6 Form of gas generator (4)
7 Damask rose essence (4)

Down

1 Maori tattoo (4)
2 Passage into mine (4)
3 (Abbr) receipt (4)
4 Movable guitar bridge (4)

Across
1 Pit or cave (3)
4 Pale blue, green paint (4)
5 To care, desire (4)
6 Goddess of all rash actions (3)

Down
1 Council, parliament (4)
2 (L) behold (4)
3 (S Afr) a col (3)
4 Undergarment (3)

Across

1 Portuguese folk-song (4)
5 (S Afr) goat (3)
6 A feast, festival (3)
7 Nest of wasps, swarm (4)

Down

2 Skilfully (4)
3 African woman's head-square (4)
4 Approval (1,1)
6 (Prefix) opposite to (2-)

Across

1 Moderately conservative (3)
4 Old Irish blood-fine (4)
6 Long, sweeping upper-cut (4)
7 Place of gross debauchery (3)

Down

1 The vexillum of a feather (3)
2 Greek god with bow (4)
3 Awning, tent (4)
5 Evasive (3)

Across

1 Prussian division of army reserve (3)
4 Rather (4)
5 To keep from (4)
6 An important date (3)

Down

1 S African Dutch (4)
2 E Indian tree, the emblic (4)
3 Catmint (3)
4 Female (3)

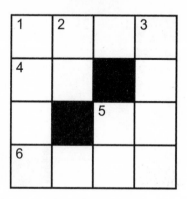

Across

1 Electronic junk mail (4)
4 ___ non troppo: but not too much (mus) (2)
5 Bishop's address (abbr) (1,1)
6 A snare, trap (4)

Down

1 Ruddle, mark on sheep (4)
2 Tannoy system (abbr) (1,1)
3 Calcareous clay (4)
5 School divinity (abbr) (1,1)

1	2	3	4
5			
6			
7			

Across

1 (Market) unofficial (4)
5 A plan (4)
6 Fish or frog spawn (4)
7 Swamp tree's root
  upgrowth (4)

Down

1 Church (4)
2 A paradise (4)
3 Counsel, advise (4)
4 Commanded (4)

Across

1 African water-antelope (3)
4 A fortified dwelling-house (4)
5 See at a distance (4)
6 The best (3)

Down

1 Sikh's uncut hair or beard (4)
2 Greek jug (4)
3 Turkish Mr (3)
4 Fondle (3)

94

Across
1 Heroin (4)
5 S Nigerian people, language (3)
6 Syrian garment (3)
7 Become entangled (4)

Down
2 Chilblain on the heel (4)
3 (Fr) down with! (1,3)
4 To be contained (2)
6 Hail Mary (abbr) (1,1)

Across

1 (Judo) One of six grades (3)
4 Auricles (4)
6 The shaft of a column (4)
7 Ground surface over a mine (3)

Down

1 State of dreamy repose (3)
2 (Scot) mare, old horse (4)
3 (L) bear (4)
5 Path, ladder (3)

Across
1 (Ger) yard, court (3)
4 (Shares) fall slightly (4)
5 Figure skating jump (4)
6 Expression of triumph (3)

Down
1 Loot from a robbery (4)
2 (Prefix) bone (4-)
3 Tarboosh (3)
4 Chess ability scale (3)

Across
1 Tibetan terrier (4)
4 American soldier (abbr) (1,1)
5 A silk (abbr) (1,1)
6 Yielding quality (4)

Down
1 Excitedly eager (4)
2 3.14159 (2)
3 Former (4)
5 As much as you wish (L) (abbr) (2)

98

Across

1 The serpent-lizard (4)
5 ___Tofana, a secret poison (4)
6 Orderly in behaviour (4)
7 ____faustus (L): lucky day (4)

Down

1 Deep-red variety of chalcedonic silica (4)
2 (Prefix) equal (4-)
3 Whimper (4)
4 Declares (4)

Across
1 A shouting, clamour (3)
4 Coal-dust (4)
5 (Fr) senior (4)
6 Bleat (3)

Down
1 New Zealand bird related to crow (4)
2 Arm bone (4)
3 (Scot) an uncle (3)
4 Ancient Hebrew capacity measure (3)

Across
1 Dogfish (4)
5 Greek letter with f-sound (3)
6 A projecting ridge (3)
7 ___ sonans (L): sounding the same (4)

Down
2 Personal music centre (1-3)
3 Clarified butter (4)
4 Judo, Karate costume (2)
6 Hello (2)

101

Across
1 Structurally unified individual creatures (3)
4 Sinks (4)
6 (Tongue) hang (4)
7 Straight line joining landscape features (3)

Down
1 Oriental cymbal (3)
2 Sixth of a drachma (4)
3 Skilled (4)
5 With hidden meaning (3)

102

Across

1 Admitting (3')
4 Viva voce (4)
5 A cul-de-sac (4)
6 Stain (3)

Down

1 Weight system for precious stones (4)
2 A gadoid fish (4)
3 (Suffix) forming names of organic compounds (-3)
4 Former (3)

103

Across

1 Drinking salutation (4)
4 For instance (abbr) (1,1)
5 Avoirdupois weight (abbr) (2)
6 'Be off!' (4)

Down

1 (Obs) since (4)
2 Metric weight (abbr) (2)
3 Timber wolf (4)
5 Behold (2)

Across

1 Polish unicameral parliament (4)
5 Floor of theatre (4)
6 (Scot) gave (4)
7 Land measure (4)

Down

1 Roman military cloaks (4)
2 ____ Clapton: rock guitarist (4)
3 Treat with derision (4)
4 Fashioned (4)

Across
1 Part of circle circumference (3)
4 Vivacity, spirit (4)
5 Luxurious establishment (4)
6 Elaborate lyric (3)

Down
1 Barren (4)
2 A liturgy (4)
3 Cousin (3)
4 Place one has great affinity with (3)

106

Across

1 Characteristic distinguishing features of bird, animal, plant (4)
5 Overly (3)
6 One-hundredth of a Rupiah (3)
7 Portent (4)

Down

2 Piece of news (4)
3 Girdle (4)
4 Yak/cow cross (2)
6 In order that (2)

Across

1 Cleopatra's slayer (3)
4 Pulley with ropes not parallel (4)
6 Ring of light (4)
7 Bill (3)

Down

1 Anti-nicotine movement (acronym) (1,1,1)
2 Move about aimlessly, gracefully (4)
3 Arrow-head (4)
5 Sailor in US Navy (3)

108

Across
1 Member of NW India, Pakistan people (3)
4 Hindu act of worship (4)
5 Part-open (4)
6 D-j (3)

Down
1 Fetish, charm (2-2)
2 A privy (4)
3 Incite to fight (3)
4 Exactly to the purpose (3)

109

Across

1 (Orkney, Shetland) springtime (4)
4 Cry of triumph (2)
5 Lodger (abbr) (1,1)
6 Fettle, fashion (4)

Down

1 Bridge-like card game (4)
2 Scots we (2)
3 Rough hard stone (4)
5 Mixed state, confusion (2)

110

1	2	3	4
5			
6			
7			

Across
1 Person of vulgar tastes (4)
5 Relating to aircraft (4)
6 Border, margin (4)
7 Threepenny bit (4)

Down
1 Go different ways (4)
2 Glass-annealing oven (4)
3 Sea-eagle (4)
4 Fulness of flavour (wine) (4)

Across
1 Lunatic asylum (3)
4 Reliable (4)
5 Lagoon separated by long sandbar (4)
6 Isle of ____, a former county (3)

Down
1 A false god (4)
2 Dubious (4)
3 Ornamental knife-rest (3)
4 Female (3)

Across
1 Hair style (4)
5 Blade (3)
6 Omission in typesetting (3)
7 Beat, thrash (4)

Down
2 ___-in-hand, a tie (4)
3 (Indonesia, Fiji) local ruler (4)
4 Before (2)
6 Take too much of drug (abbr) (1,1)

Across
1 Scion (3)
4 Indian weight (4)
6 Hindu festival, fair (4)
7 A lump, blow, thump (3)

Down
1 Distinctive theory (3)
2 Reward (4)
3 White wax (4)
5 Excellent, admirably up to date (3)

114

Across
1 Fur, feather coil (3)
4 A Japanese people, language (4)
5 Driving mist (4)
6 Suffix denoting country of origin (-3)

Down
1 Prejudice unfairly (4)
2 As soon as (4)
3 Seabird (3)
4 100 sq m (3)

Across

1 Bloodhound's pendulous upper lip (4)
4 Egyptian sun-god (2)
5 To cook (2)
6 (Spenser) go, proceed (4)

Down

1 A brawl (4)
2 Hollywood city (abbr) (1,1)
3 Cask as storage for wine (4)
5 Burmese knife (2)

116

1	2	3	4
5			
6			
7			

Across

1 Hold position against current (4)
5 S American spotted cavy (4)
6 In continuing pain (4)
7 Cycle of duty (4)

Down

1 Rafter, pole (4)
2 Mexican pancake (4)
3 Authentic (4)
4 S American Indian people (4)

117

Across
1 Make out, discover (3)
4 To drag (4)
5 Came to rest (4)
6 Umbrella-shaped dagoba finial (3)

Down
1 Sallow (4)
2 Ballet movement (4)
3 At the same time (3)
4 Office of cardinal (3)

118

Across
1 French priest (4)
5 In excess, wonderful (3)
6 Past (3)
7 Indian groom (4)

Down
2 Goblin (4)
3 Combination of nations (4)
4 One in charge of periodical (abbr) (2)
6 To that extent (2)

119

Across
1 Plant of meadow-grass genus (3)
4 Cancel, annul (4)
6 Member of the pig family (4)
7 Distance phone system (abbr) (1,1,1)

Down
1 Suppuration fluid (3)
2 Responsibility (4)
3 Opening, passage (4)
5 Standing apart (3)

Across

1 (Prescriptions) in equal quantities (3)
4 Turn about the axis (4)
5 Grow sound (4)
6 A sixth sense (abbr) (1,1,1)

Down

1 Feasts, festivals (4)
2 (Tide) a small range (4)
3 Pointed instrument (3)
4 Eponymous pronoun (3)

	1	2		3
	4		■	
		■	5	
	6			

Across
1 Tidal bore (4)
4 Symbol for plutonium (2)
5 'It' (abbr) (1,1)
6 An alcohol radical (4)

Down
1 Ancient dry goods measure (4)
2 Shetland viol (2)
3 Iran, Oman currency unit (4)
5 (Prefix) together (2-)

122

1	2	3	4
5			
6			
7			

Across
1 Variety of id (4)
5 Guffaw (4)
6 A fish-roe (4)
7 'Old News' Queen (4)

Down
1 (Scot) odd (4)
2 Grained sheepskin leather (4)
3 Yellowish brown (4)
4 Sea-eagle (4)

123

	1	2	3
4			
5			
6			■

Across

1 To put in order (3)
4 Mopoke (4)
5 Farsi its official language (4)
6 Tending to (3)

Down

1 Small hook-like piton (4)
2 The E of QEF (4)
3 Hill, fortified mound (3)
4 Drowned valley (3)

124

Across

1 Korean verse form (4)
5 ___ in urbe: town's rural atmosphere (3)
6 British rule in India (3)
7 ____ vitae: brandy (4)

Down

2 Mesopotamia (4)
3 Fetish, charm (4)
4 Exceptionally large (abbr) (2)
6 Academician (abbr) (1,1)

125

Across
1 Second tine of deer's horn (3)
4 (Shakesp) clamour, din (4)
6 Division of Sussex (4)
7 Tyre pressure measurement (1,1,1)

Down
1 Murmur, whisper hoarsely (3)
2 Nipa, palm (4)
3 Golfers' nervous trembling (4)
5 Kind of rorqual (3)

126

Across

1 A gypsy (3)
4 Whimper (4)
5 Lop, prune (4)
6 34th US president (3)

Down

1 Touchwood (4)
2 Toward sheltered side (4)
3 Closely unite (3)
4 ____ phenomena, those of parapsychology (3)

Across

1 Aircraft wheel fairing (4)
4 Former partner (2)
5 Cry of pain (2)
6 Chances, probability (4)

Down

1 Showy liliaceous plant (4)
2 American services overseas shop (abbr) (1,1)
3 Leather strap for punishment (4)
5 Reichenbach force (2)

Across

1 Square pattern of tartan (4)
5 S African weaver bird (4)
6 Second largest city of Algeria (4)
7 To stake, pay (up) (4)

Down

1 Covered colonnade (4)
2 (Milk) curdle (4)
3 To such a degree (4)
4 The___ (Scot): That one (4)

129

Across
1 En tout ____: parasol/ umbrella (3)
4 Intention, purpose (4)
5 In plentiful supply (4)
6 Signaller's T (3)

Down
1 Hi or Bye (4)
2 An OE rune (4)
3 Australian game of two-up (3)
4 Examine critically (3)

130

Across
1 (Bible) worthless (4)
5 Doomed, fated to die soon (3)
6 A native Chinese (3)
7 Formerly (4)

Down
2 At a distance (4)
3 (Fr Can) annual nominal payment to property owner (4)
4 Oh! Alas! (2)
6 Male (2)

Across

1 Sink (3)
4 Second section of scherzo etc (4)
6 Haunch, hip (4)
7 Type of shirt (3)

Down

1 Barred D (3)
2 (Wine) unsweetened (4)
3 Pale blue or green paint (4)
5 Turkish weight (3)

Across
1 Spurious, base (3)
4 A temple (4)
5 Vain (4)
6 Miniature breed (3)

Down
1 Cubic body of pedestal (4)
2 Barely (4)
3 Radio-navigation system (3)
4 A canto (3)

Across

1 Offhand (4)
4 (They) made it (L) (abbr) (2)
5 Win or place (abbr) (1,1)
6 Barks sharply (4)

Down

1 (Obs) to trust (4)
2 Provided that (2)
3 Button scurvy (4)
5 Type of record (abbr) (1,1)

134

1	2	3	4
5			
6			
7			

Across
1 Recess at end of choir (4)
5 Badly-behaved child (4)
6 Permission to use (4)
7 First mortal (Hindu) (4)

Down
1 With skill (4)
2 Malay boat (4)
3 A Lapp (4)
4 Liquid-heating sauces (4)

Across

1 In____: asunder (3)
4 Crucifix (4)
5 Gumbo (4)
6 Horseradish tree (3)

Down

1 Puff on marijuana cigarette (4)
2 Effete (4)
3 Room in harem (3)
4 Fruit syrup (3)

136

Across
1 Lymph node swelling (4)
5 ___vomica, strychnine yielding tree (3)
6 Wine stand (3)
7 (Fr) state, rank (4)

Down
2 One (4)
3 Artificial rubber (4)
4 Bovine animal (2)
6 Take place (2)

Across
1 A bomb (3)
4 (Dialect) to worry (4)
6 A balsam (4)
7 School of whales (3)

Down
1 Newt (3)
2 Spirits and waters (4)
3 Festivity (4)
5 Murmur like a bee (3)

138

Across
1 A computer programming language (3)
4 Push aside (4)
5 Liquor of tan vat (4)
6 Side issue (3)

Down
1 Nautical hail (4)
2 Be half-asleep (4)
3 To mature (3)
4 Weep noisily (3)

Across

1 Kingfish (4)
4 Cook (2)
5 Expression of surprise (2)
6 Type of aircraft (acronym) (4)

Down

1 Chances, probability (4)
2 Gazunder (2)
3 (Welsh) emotional fervour (4)
5 Way of working (abbr) (1,1)

1	2	3	4
5			
6			
7			

Across
1 Empty speechifying (4)
5 Carbamide (4)
6 Inner door grating (4)
7 Inclination from the vertical (4)

Down
1 German river, industrial region (4)
2 Superficial extent (4)
3 An isthmus (4)
4 Successful tissue graft (4)

141

Across
1 Corroded (3)
4 Silk yarn for weft (4)
5 (Am) country bumpkin (4)
6 A friend (3)

Down
1 Wake-robin (4)
2 Sock worn with Japanese sandals (4)
3 Moon bounce (1,1,1)
4 (Prefix) across (3-)

142

1	**2**	**3**	**4**
	5		
6			
7			

Across
1 Periodic payment of rent (4)
5 Wire diameter measure (3)
6 (Oxbridge) outer door (3)
7 Bodily quality (4)

Down
2 Native maidservant (4)
3 Exact resemblance (4)
4 (Am) overhead railway (2)
6 Bible part (abbr) (1,1)

Across

1 Nail obliquely through the foot (3)
4 In the manner of (dutch etc) (4)
6 Hawaiian goose (4)
7 Additional (3)

Down

1 Large cask (3)
2 Unfrozen (4)
3 OE domestic slave (4)
5 Tree with elastic wood (3)

Across

1 Company performing a dance (3)
4 Advance payment (4)
5 Blunder (4)
6 Growth from a glume (3)

Down

1 'Cocaine' (4)
2 College suit (4)
3 Ethiopian cereal grass (3)
4 Kitchen stove (3)

145

Across

1 Thoroughly (4)
4 Kung ___, a martial art (2)
5 Building wing (2)
6 Trek in a laboured way (4)

Down

1 Risky (4)
2 Greek letter written v (2)
3 Sharp cry (4)
5 ___ dash; wide dash (Printing) (2)

146

1	2	3	4
5			
6			
7			

Across

1 Indian, Carib cake of unleavened bread (4)
5 During (4)
6 A mainly terrestrial tree shrew (4)
7 Toward the sheltered side (4)

Down

1 A canon (4)
2 Surrey ground (4)
3 Injury, affliction (4)
4 Dies ____ : judgement day (4)

Across

1 A proprietary germicide (abbr) (1,1,1)
4 Bronze Age trumpet (4)
5 (Scot) mare, old horse (4)
6 An outer district (3)

Down

1 Wambenger (4)
2 Radioactive waste (4)
3 Hamper, pannier (3)
4 Solution obtained by leaching (3)

Across

1 Pulpit, reading-desk (4)
5 Familiar, accustomed (3)
6 Tangle (seaweed) (3)
7 Dressing-gown (4)

Down

2 Philippine Muslim tribe member (4)
3 Blister, bubble (4)
4 Reichenbach force (2)
6 Non-officers (military) (abbr) (1,1)

Across
1 Snake (3)
4 Two-syllable foot (4)
6 Delay, hinder (4)
7 Haggard novel (3)

Down
1 (Music) twice (3)
2 Cereal grass (4)
3 Native children's nurse (4)
5 A side issue (3)

Across

1 (Spenser) a river (3)
4 A polio vaccine (4)
5 Actual existence (4)
6 Corroded (3)

Down

1 Cobbler's foot model (4)
2 Besides (4)
3 Make up required measure (3)
4 The tide (3)

Across
1 Polynesian demigod (4)
4 (Ger) for example (abbr) (1,1)
5 Batting (2)
6 Nothingness (4)

Down
1 Muslim call to prayer (4)
2 In the same place (L) (abbr) (2)
3 Arm bone (4)
5 Freshwater fish (2)

152

1	2	3	4
5			
6			
7			

Across
1 Southernmost Israeli city (4)
5 Type of ferry (2-2)
6 A squirrel (4)
7 Sieve, strainer (4)

Down
1 Formerly (4)
2 Short, narrow lane (4)
3 Wake-robin (4)
4 Clothing (4)

153

Across
1 Extinct bird (3)
4 Course thread in lace-making (4)
5 Dismounted (4)
6 A dram (3)

Down
1 Drought-resistant variety of sorghum (4)
2 Fail to use (4)
3 Appropriate (3)
4 Opening between sandbanks (3)

154

Across
1 Biblical to (4)
5 Crass-witted person (3)
6 Time just before event (3)
7 Fertilizer clay (4)

Down
2 Suddenly brighter star (4)
3 Rank (4)
4 Satisfactory (1,1)
6 13th letter (2)

155

1	**2**	**3**	■
4			**5**
6			
■	**7**		

Across
1 Nipple (3)
4 A portion of surface (4)
6 Membrane, caul (4)
7 Etched (3)

Down
1 (India) mail (3)
2 Carbamide (4)
3 (Am) money (4)
5 Old feast (3)

Across
1 (Scot) friend (3)
4 At all, possibly (4)
5 Group of families (4)
6 Large antelope (3)

Down
1 So much as (4)
2 List of possible options (4)
3 Bitter vetch (3)
4 Gamete (3)

Across

1 Discount on foreign bill of exchange (4)
4 Provided (2)
5 Doh (2)
6 Golfer's trembling fit (4)

Down

1 Like dust (4)
2 Energy (2)
3 Pastoral songs (4)
5 Risen (2)

1	2	3	4
5			
6			
7			

Across

1 Ship's gangway (4)
5 Side piece of wagon (4)
6 Seaweed jelly (4)
7 Mythical tusked horse (4)

Down

1 Pound in mortar (4)
2 Melodic pattern in Hindu music (4)
3 Round at both ends (4)
4 Used to be (4)

159

Across
1 (Wine) dry (3)
4 A literal (print) (4)
5 Response (4)
6 Fallow (3)

Down
1 Indian groom (4)
2 One tenth of a Homer (4)
3 Murmur softly (3)
4 Hill, mound in Arab lands (3)

160

Across

1 Trading place (4)
5 Small deer (3)
6 Image of self (3)
7 Theatre gallery (4)

Down

2 Large southern constellation (4)
3 Crucifix (4)
4 ___igitur: thee, therefore (2)
6 By way of example (abbr) (1,1)

161

Across
1 Indian state (3)
4 In the year (4)
6 A hogshead (4)
7 Government assessment of local authority funds (1,1,1)

Down
1 Tusk (3)
2 Burden (4)
3 Black cuckoos (4)
5 Room in harem (3)

Across
1 She-badger (3)
4 Pasta like short-cut macaroni (4)
5 To issue (4)
6 Coccid insect resin (3)

Down
1 Earth's crust below sial (4)
2 Of the ear (4)
3 To know (3)
4 Oriental cymbal (3)

163

1	**2**		**3**
4		■	
	■	**5**	
6			

Across
1 (Shakesp) equal (4)
4 Maori digging stick (2)
5 On the spot (2)
6 Short religious drama (4)

Down
1 Small Indian carriage (4)
2 A spell, turn (2)
3 Thin muslin-like fabric (4)
5 Information Technology (2)

¹	²	³	⁴
⁵			
⁶			
⁷			

Across

1 Tease out, comb (4)
5 The cheek; a molar (4)
6 Piece of news (4)
7 The tea genus (4)

Down

1 A foolishly annoying person (4)
2 A curse (4)
3 (Obs) to cut (4)
4 Costard's version of 'enigma' (4)

165

Across
1 Stage of a journey (3)
4 A chink (4)
5 Alcohol radical (4)
6 Something delightful (3)

Down
1 A whitish bean (4)
2 A genus of terrapins (4)
3 A unit of acceleration (3)
4 Pithy part of orange etc (3)

166

Across

1 Large number, heap (4)
5 In favour of (3)
6 (Horse) move to the right (3)
7 Hedge with rail, ditch jump (4)

Down

2 Tip (4)
3 Lavish (4)
4 Close against (2)
6 Elapse (2)

¹	²	³	■
⁴			⁵
⁶			
■	⁷		

Across
1 Invite (3)
4 Scottish chief herald (4)
6 Square pilaster by doorway (4)
7 (Austr) inform on (3)

Down
1 In the manner of (1,2)
2 To wash, rinse out (4)
3 Japanese stringed instrument (4)
5 A hilltop, promontory (3)

168

Across
1 Weak, feeble (3)
4 (India) a newly-formed island (4)
5 Weird (4)
6 An outer district (3)

Down
1 While (4)
2 Yird (4)
3 Annoy, irritate (3)
4 Type of carriage spring (3)

Across
1 River bore (4)
4 Therefore (2)
5 On horseback (2)
6 Ready; manageable (4)

Down
1 To observe (4)
2 An attempt (2)
3 Division of Sussex (4)
5 (Prefix) primitive (2-)

170

1	2	3	4
5			
6			
7			

Across
1 Remained fixed (4)
5 Muslim prince's title (4)
6 Abounding (4)
7 (Cards) three (4)

Down
1 Male deer (4)
2 N African Chieftain (4)
3 Conscious existence (4)
4 Squirrel's nest (4)

Across
1 Toss (3)
4 Fencing sword (4)
5 Gull genus (4)
6 Ovine female (3)

Down
1 Ooze, run (4)
2 Pigment in blood (4)
3 Indeed (3)
4 Devon river (3)

Across

1 Symbol of life (4)
5 '...floats on high ___ vales and hills' (Wordsworth) (3)
6 Badly (3)
7 A natural occurring amino acid (4)

Down

2 ___episcopari: refusal of responsible position (4)
3 Wrack (4)
4 US lower house (abbr) (1,1)
6 One of three parts of the personality (2)

173

Across
1 Solemn person (3)
4 Scene (4)
6 Polygonal recess (4)
7 (Scot) eyes (3)

Down
1 Female gametes (3)
2 Erase tape (4)
3 ___-majesty: treason (4)
5 Sebaceous cyst (3)

Across

1 Vintage (3)
4 A court of record (4)
5 Baseless (4)
6 Algiers governor (3)

Down

1 Give way (4)
2 Depend confidently (4)
3 A N American Indian
people (3)
4 'Hat' (3)

Across
1 An imbalance (4)
4 Just after (2)
5 Hold true (2)
6 Figure skating jump (4)

Down
1 NE wind in the Adriatic (4)
2 On good terms with (2)
3 Drinking salutation (4)
5 Greek earth goddess (2)

176

1	2	3	4
5			
6			
7			

Across
1 Supplicate (4)
5 Side of bird's head (4)
6 Indigo (4)
7 Dark greenish-blue colour (4)

Down
1 Flat region (4)
2 (Scot) A roof-gutter (4)
3 Accompanied vocal solo (4)
4 Sharp cry (4)

Across
1 Noise intensity measure (3)
4 To put on board (4)
5 Seaweed (4)
6 Former pasha of Algiers (3)

Down
1 Bundle, package (4)
2 Nervous (4)
3 Fallow (3)
4 Stableman (3)

178

Across
1 Soul, essence (It) (4)
5 Charged particle (3)
6 Seek (3)
7 Coping of a gable (4)

Down
2 Groin, flank (4)
3 Donkey (4)
4 If (2)
6 Roman pound (2)

179

Across

1 Wreath of flowers, shells (3)
4 Book of Scandinavian mythology (4)
6 Salmon that has just spawned (4)
7 (Spenser) is not (3)

Down

1 Game bird display season (3)
2 A paradise (4)
3 In an off hand way (4)
5 (Law) at the suit of (abbr) (3)

Across
1 Habitual joker (3)
4 Wild mango tree (4)
5 Greek god of war (4)
6 Radio-navigation system (3)

Down
1 A pickpocket (4)
2 Small African/Caribbean fruit tree (4)
3 Frothy talk (3)
4 Dirt-clotted tuft of wool (3)

Across
1 Coal dust (4)
4 Sweet vermouth (2)
5 So far (2)
6 Thin fabric like muslin (4)

Down
1 Timber at base of window opening (4)
2 ____dictum: as said (2)
3 Soya bean paste (4)
5 In the year (L) (abbr) (2)

182

Across
1 Personal belongings (4)
5 Portoferraio its chief town (4)
6 Dirty woman (4)
7 9th letter of Hebrew alphabet (4)

Down
1 Tale of adventure, romance (4)
2 French she (4)
3 To border (4)
4 Prehistoric hill fort (4)

Across
1 Yarn measure (3)
4 A fibre of flax (4)
5 To calm (4)
6 The best (3)

Down
1 Daughter of Laban (4)
2 Irish Gaelic (4)
3 Feast, festival (3)
4 Heated (3)

184

Across

1 3rd stage of Alpine glaciation (4)
5 See 6 down (3)
6 High tone (3)
7 As assize (4)

Down

2 In an offhand way (4)
3 To glut (4)
4 Scientific units system (1,1)
6, 5 ac. Traditional Vietnamese tunic (2,3)

Across
1 Knowing (3)
4 Muslim potentate (4)
6 Agave fibre (4)
7 Vietnamese festival (3)

Down
1 Render melancholy (3)
2 Issue (4)
3 Crown of head (4)
5 Web of rope yarn (3)

Across
1 Health resort (3)
4 Relating to a wing (4)
5 Muslim market (4)
6 Nutritious seed (3)

Down
1 Blackthorn bush (4)
2 New Zealand abalone (4)
3 Coffer (3)
4 Cleopatra's snake (3)

Across
1 A party (4)
4 A mouth, mouth-like opening (2)
5 (Russ) yes (2)
6 Tip, point (4)

Down
1 (Afr) a fenced enclosure (4)
2 Norse god (2)
3 practical joke (4)
5 ___ facto: actually (2)

188

1	2	3	4
5			
6			
7			

Across
1 Mineral springs (4)
5 St Columba's monastery island (4)
6 Decayed wood as tinder (4)
7 Branching stand (4)

Down
1 Investigate item by item (___through) (4)
2 Proceed in profusion (4)
3 'Dead' Queen (4)
4 Fermented rice drink (4)

Across
1 Rag, piece of cloth (3)
4 Queensland hemp genus (4)
5 Indefinite (4)
6 Before (3)

Down
1 Ananias (4)
2 Cutting tool (4)
3 Smear with tar (3)
4 Female (3)

Across
1 A Chinese dynasty (4)
5 A marsupial (3)
6 Stir, bustle (3)
7 Small S African antelope (4)

Down
2 Pakistani language (4)
3 Formerly, ninth hour of the day (4)
4 Be regarded as (2)
6 Roman weight (2)

191

Across

1 Alias (abbr) (1,1,1)
4 A QC (4)
6 Black (4)
7 ____captain: an
   obsequious attendant (3)

Down

1 Fool (3)
2 (Print) cut (4)
3 Shrub, tree of lily family (4)
5 Wingless fly (3)

Across

1 Involuntary habitual response (3)
4 Old-fashioned or stupid person (4)
5 In a proficient way (4)
6 Strong alkaline solution (3)

Down

1 Robbery on the road (4)
2 Tick over (4)
3 Evasive (3)
4 Pigeon pea (3)

193

Across

1 Guy-rope to steady gaff (4)
4 (L) (abbr) died (2)
5 Because in that case (2)
6 Prevalent (4)

Down

1 Orkney, Shetland springtime (4)
2 Naval rating (1,1)
3 A spiral turn (4)
5 Made from (2)

Across

1 (Scot, law) stop, stay (4)
5 Affectedly artistic (4)
6 Unrefined cane sugar (4)
7 Advance payment (4)

Down

1 A body of legend (4)
2 Inflexible (4)
3 Bullock, steer (4)
4 Rubber tube (4)

Across
1 Gone (3)
4 (Am) fit of bad temper (4)
5 An instrumental tune (4)
6 A computer logic circuit (3)

Down
1 Coming! (4)
2 Encompass, surround (4)
3 Excessive (abbr) (1,1,1)
4 Pool of aerated water (3)

Across

1 Blackleg (4)
5 Central American rubber tree (3)
6 A fairy (3)
7 Arabian sultanate (4)

Down

2 Stem of grass (4)
3 N African esparto grass (4)
4 Occupy a position in space (2)
6 18th c gambling game (1,1)

197

Across
1 A region (3)
4 Scowl (4)
6 Three point score in judo (4)
7 (Scot) matted wool (3)

Down
1 Largest deer (3)
2 Secluded retreat (4)
3 The fist (4)
5 A renegade (3)

198

Across
1 A hollow (3)
4 Croatian monetary unit (4)
5 Knitwear style (4)
6 Motion through the water (3)

Down
1 Turkish monetary unit (4)
2 (Archaic) satisfy (4)
3 Betel nut (3)
4 Mosaic code (3)

Across

1 An ornamental soft rosette (4)
4 Behold (2)
5 Take place (2)
6 Malay boat (4)

Down

1 Horse's hoof sound (4)
2 Hullo (2)
3 Pigment-bearing layer of eye (4)
5 Pipal tree (2)

200

Across
1 Male turkey-cock (4)
5 Oleaginous (4)
6 A gripping instrument (4)
7 Central tower (4)

Down
1 A ploughshare (4)
2 Mah-jongg piece (4)
3 Winglike processes (4)
4 Coarse lace-making thread (4)

201

Across
1 Poor, rotten (3)
4 Punishment (4)
5 A curse (4)
6 Important date (3)

Down
1 Male pig (4)
2 Official minutes (4)
3 First note of scale (3)
4 Stand against starting-line (3)

202

Across
1 Skilled (4)
5 Criminal charge (3)
6 Mien (3)
7 Maori tattoo (4)

Down
2 Vivacity (4)
3 Play about (4)
4 45 rpm record (abbr) (1,1)
6 Hail Mary (abbr) (1,1)

Across

1 Current unit (abbr) (3)
4 Sound from diseased lung (4)
6 Of W Indian witchcraft (4)
7 At all (3)

Down

1 Make bomb ready (3)
2 Illusion (4)
3 Intended method (4)
5 A holy see (3)

204

Across
1 Inquire after (3)
4 Malaria (4)
5 Bloody (4)
6 A joke; a drink (3)

Down
1 Ancient Greek contest (4)
2 Without possibility (4)
3 Ash fruit (3)
4 Since (3)

205

Across
1 Examine by touch (4)
4 Grandchild (2)
5 Group of Chinese dialects (2)
6 Court of record held in ____ (4)

Down
1 Taking of vote (4)
2 Oh; alas (2)
3 The bib (fish) (4)
5 People in general (2)

206

1	2	3	4
5			
6			
7			

Across
1 Boring (4)
5 Dance energetically (4)
6 (L) to be (4)
7 That which (4)

Down
1 Small duck (4)
2 (scot) lord (4)
3 Bones (4)
4 Make keen (4)

207

Across
1 A side issue (3)
4 To crumble (4)
5 To make good (4)
6 Gladstone; elderly, venerated person (abbr) (1,1,1)

Down
1 Lymph node swelling (4)
2 Substance from which elements developed (4)
3 English language teaching (1,1,1)
4 To chatter, to tease (3)

208

Across

1 Swindle (4)
5 Expression of triumph (3)
6 Grey-brown Tibetan gazelle (3)
7 Mate (4)

Down

2 A wicker basket (4)
3 Introductory section of a raga (4)
4 Chronic fatigue syndrome (abbr) (1,1)
6 Hold true (2)

209

Across
1 Mouth-like openings (3)
4 Forsaken (4)
6 A raincoat of hemp (4)
7 The tag end (3)

Down
1 Cave dwelling salamander (3)
2 Move turbulently (4)
3 Indian water buffalo (4)
5 A stump, snag (3)

210

Across

1 Plant of meadow grass genus (3)
4 Coarse-ground maize (4)
5 Got off vehicle (4)
6 Unit of luminance (3)

Down

1 Buddhist sacred language (4)
2 Fail to use (4)
3 Ready, prone (3)
4 Japanese Mr, Mrs (3)

211

Across
1 Horn of the moon (4)
4 Dominicans (L) (abbr) (1,1)
5 Accomplish (2)
6 Flock of larks (4)

Down
1 Honey store (4)
2 Amiss (2)
3 Game manoeuvre (4)
5 God willing (L) (abbr) (1,1)

1	**2**	**3**	**4**
5			
6			
7			

Across
1 Engaged in (2,2)
5 Miner's compass (4)
6 Barren (4)
7 A monocotyledon (4)

Down
1 Allodial (4)
2 (Repeated) spicy sauce (4-)
3 Inheritance limitation (4)
4 Song, etc, from the past (4)

Across
1 Snake genus (3)
4 (N Ireland) a Catholic (4)
5 An eagle (4)
6 (India) travel by relays (3)

Down
1 ____ brith: a Welsh fruit bread (4)
2 Pig sound (4)
3 Century (3)
4 Spread grass to dry (3)

214

1	2	3	4
	5		
6			
7			

Across
1 Sound flatter than plop (4)
5 (L) where (3)
6 S American wood sorrel (3)
7 A col (4)

Down
2 Pike (4)
3 A nomogram (4)
4 Obtrusively religious (2)
6 Being shown (2)

Across
1 (Scot) wooden drinking-bowl (3)
4 In elaborate lyric form (4)
6 (India) spiritual father (4)
7 Type of sleep (abbr) (1,1,1)

Down
1 Sower's wicker basket (3)
2 Jewish month (4)
3 Butt of wine (4)
5 Combined with (3)

216

Across

1 Cubical part of pedestal (3)
4 1 lumen per sq cm (4)
5 RC supreme ecclesiastical tribunal (4)
6 Highest pitch (1-2)

Down

1 Indian drum (4)
2 Very small amount (4)
3 Greek long e (3)
4 (Prefix) anterior part (3-)

217

Across
1 Mettle (4)
4 Laos monetary unit (2)
5 Liechtenstein (abbr) (2)
6 (Scot) selected list of candidates (4)

Down
1 Catch engaging with ratchet (4)
2 The ne plus ultra (2)
3 Otter's den (4)
5 Auto-da- __: public burning (2)

1	2	3	4
5			
6			
7			

Across
1 Official minutes (4)
5 To starve (4)
6 ____ pad, a landing-place (4)
7 Old mild oath (4)

Down
1 Long for (4)
2 A gadfly (4)
3 Web (4)
4 In the midst of (4)

219

	1	2	3
4			
5			
6			

Across
1 Revenons à ___ moutons: back to business (3)
4 Hindu festival, fair (4)
5 Irish blood-fine (4)
6 Japanese species of Aralia (3)

Down
1 Geek (4)
2 Savoury dish, medley (4)
3 Pouch (3)
4 Baldmoney, spignel (3)

220

1	2	3	4
	5		
6			
7			

Across
1 Bent-knees ballet position (4)
5 Charged particle (3)
6 To decline (3)
7 Son of Judah (4)

Down
2 Right of property retention (4)
3 Jot (4)
4 Half an em (2)
6 In a high degree (2)

221

1	2	3	
4			5
6			
	7		

Across
1 Meadow-grass genus (3)
4 Rice-shaped pasta (4)
6 A reef in the sea (4)
7 Pismire (3)

Down
1 Chambers (3)
2 Black and white whale (4)
3 Muslim call to prayer (4)
5 Food scrap (3)

Across
1 An uncle (3)
4 Ellipsoidal (4)
5 Paper size (4)
6 Rugby support for dead ball (3)

Down
1 Bacchic cry (4)
2 Paraguay tea (4)
3 Test measuring fibrinolysis (1,1,1)
4 Make a choice (3)

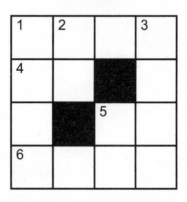

Across
1 Species of skunk (4)
4 A beloved (2)
5 __ that: moreover (2)
6 Genus of gulls (4)

Down
1 A privy (4)
2 In contact with (2)
3 Formal karate practice (4)
5 US MA (1,1)

1	2	3	4
5			
6			
7			

Across
1 Cabbage salad (4)
5 Aromatic plant of pepper family (4)
6 Continual enjoyment of a right (4)
7 A first principle (4)

Down
1 Squirrel (4)
2 Be crystal for monochromatic light (4)
3 Allege in pleading (4)
4 Become ardent (4)

225

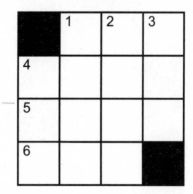

Across
1 Silver coin of ancient Palestine (3)
4 To whimper (4)
5 Not fully decided (4)
6 Make heavy demands on (3)

Down
1 Serbian confederation of villages (4)
2 Gorse genus (4)
3 Japanese Buddhism (3)
4 Deep hole in limestone (3)

226

Across
1 Fish related to herring (4)
5 Auxiliary international language (3)
6 Travel on snow (3)
7 Paving-block (4)

Down
2 Suddenly increase prices (4)
3 Mine passage (4)
4 A hoax (2)
6 Nazi elite corps (abbr) (1,1)

227

Across
1 To supplement (3)
4 The mere pleasure of playing (4)
6 A dry watercourse, ravine (4)
7 One event in contest (3)

Down
1 N European moose (3)
2 Black eye powder (4)
3 Cry of Bacchic frenzy (4)
5 Unit of work (3)

228

Across
1 The weather (3)
4 In India, tea (4)
5 A stirrup (4)
6 Plug, socket standard system (1,1,1)

Down
1 Indian male address (4)
2 Type of subatomic particle (4)
3 Opposing principle of yang (3)
4 Chief, hero (3)

Across
1 Betting price (4)
4 Aged (abbr) (2)
5 Small Pacific liliaceous tree (2)
6 Pilchard fishermen's lookout man (4)

Down
1 A curse (4)
2 __ Profundis (Oscar Wilde) (2)
3 Make gathers in (4)
5 __ igitur, service-book (2)

1	2	3	4
5			
6			
7			

Across
1 Smoky obscurity (4)
5 Of the dawn (4)
6 Large E Indian deer (4)
7 Obsolete 'fetch' (4)

Down
1 A villein (4)
2 Grimace of discontent (4)
3 Malt kiln (4)
4 Mosquito (4)

Across
1 Hawthorn blossom (3)
4 Innermost part (4)
5 Resistance measures (4)
6 Examine critically (3)

Down
1 W African gazelle (4)
2 Host (4)
3 Indeed (3)
4 Hospital bed (3)

232

Across

1 ____ dixit: he himself said it (4)
5 Slack (3)
6 The jack of clubs (3)
7 A literal (mistake in print) (4)

Down

2 Action of wielding (4)
3 Coarse maize porridge (4)
4 Direct from (2)
6 Gym (abbr) (1,1)

Across
1 Namely (abbr) (3)
4 Hard, black, stone-like (wood) (4)
6 A volley, broadside (4)
7 Angle between horizontal and earth's magnetic field (3)

Down
1 Examine and pass (3)
2 In the same place (L) (abbr) (4)
3 Japanese sandal (4)
5 Catmint (3)

234

	1	2	3
4			
5			
6			

Across

1 Support garment (3)
4 (Equine) give birth (4)
5 Except that mentioned (4)
6 Barred D (3)

Down

1 Uncut edge of sheet folded for book (4)
2 Over-hasty (4)
3 Alcoholic beverage (3)
4 Feudal tenure (3)

Across
1 A long time (4)
4 Stop (2)
5 Government tax
   department (abbr) (1,1)
6 'Young people' (4)

Down
1 Nautical hail (4)
2 Energy (2)
3 One in modified slavery (4)
5 Expression of joy or grief (2)

1	2	3	4
5			
6			
7			

Across
1 ____ vult: Crusaders' cry (4)
5 Strongly advise (4)
6 Gangster's girlfriend (4)
7 Expression of incredulity (2,2)

Down
1 Russian parliament (4)
2 Asteroid discovered 1898 (4)
3 Grapefruit/orange/tangerine cross (4)
4 Personality (4)

237

Across
1 Steam bath establishment (3)
4 Indian oil-yielding tree (4)
5 St Columba's monastery island (4)
6 Some (3)

Down
1 Willingly (4)
2 £25 (4)
3 Literary anecdotes (3)
4 Tropical plant yielding arrow root (3)

Across

1 Unbleached linen (4)
5 Heated (3)
6 House, farm in S of France (3)
7 Attar (4)

Down

2 Small, poor quality potato (4)
3 Interval of silence (music) (4)
4 Doh (2)
6 Instant (2)

239

Across
1 Form of Jamaican music (3)
4 Thread of a screw (4)
6 System of Hindu philosophy (4)
7 African waterbuck (3)

Down
1 Australian game of two-up (3)
2 Mad, eccentric person (4)
3 Jason's ship (4)
5 Queen of the fairies (3)

240

Across
1 Numbers (abbr) (3)
4 To vomit (4)
5 State of agitation (4)
6 Flying saucer (abbr) (1,1,1)

Down
1 Ingenuous (4)
2 Pasta in barley-like pieces (4)
3 (Mus) forced with sudden emphasis (abbr) (3)
4 1 kWh (abbr) (1,1,1)

241

Across
1 Sepulchral monument (4)
4 Amiss (2)
5 Judo, karate costume (2)
6 Shoot at young partridges, grouse (4)

Down
1 Hillock, mound (4)
2 One side of stage (2)
3 To harass (4)
5 Former Shetland viol (2)

242

1	2	3	4
5			
6			
7			

Across
1 Roman military cloaks (4)
5 Cameo agate (4)
6 The front (4)
7 Chinese ounce (4)

Down
1 Piano (4)
2 Sapi-utan (4)
3 A ring, circle (4)
4 Ice skating jump (4)

243

Across

1 ___-Magnon, of early homo sapiens (3)
4 ____ populi: the mob (4)
5 Discover unexpectedly (4)
6 Correct a computer fault (3)

Down

1 House, mansion (4)
2 Corded cloth (4)
3 (Prefixed) oxygen (3-)
4 Tarboosh (3)

244

Across
1 Engaged in (2,2)
5 Sweep (3)
6 Electrically charged particle (3)
7 Secure by many turns of lashing (4)

Down
2 To be pitied (4)
3 Indian military, police station (4)
4 Alternative link (2)
6 Supposing that (2)

1	2	3	
4			5
6			
	7		

Across
1 It shows maiden name (3)
4 Cereal seeds (4)
6 A pellicle of ice (4)
7 Dismounted (3)

Down
1 Stump, snag (3)
2 ____ Marshal, president of Heralds' College (4)
3 Sewing articles case (4)
5 To hang in position (3)

Across

1 Ring of metal forming handle (3)
4 Sound contented (4)
5 (Obs) to trust 4)
6 She-antelope (3)

Down

1 (Jonson) black tincture in alchemy (4)
2 Golden-yellow fish (4)
3 Sardonic (3)
4 Foot of hunted animal (3)

247

Across
1 Personal opinion newspaper feature (2-2)
4 Rugger (abbr) (1,1)
5 Three-toed sloth (2)
6 Open colonnade (4)

Down
1 Antelope (4)
2 Symbol for plutonium (2)
3 Thing of no value (4)
5 So far (2)

1	2	3	4
5			
6			
7			

Across

1 Act of trumping (4)
5 External occipital protuberances (4)
6 Come upon game (4)
7 Enemies (4)

Down

1 Phrase played repeatedly (4)
2 Pearl mussel genus (4)
3 French brandy (4)
4 Passing hobbies (4)

249

Across
1 Gull (3)
4 Rounding-off musical section (4)
5 Descended (4)
6 Opinion, guess (3)

Down
1 Mexican chilli, chocolate sauce (4)
2 Bowdlerize (4)
3 A hare (3)
4 Hebrew capacity measure (3)

250

Across

1 Eastern corner of Arabia (4)
5 Five-frame piece (3)
6 American Indian; Australian truck (3)
7 Honey-buzzard (4)

Down

2 Boundary (4)
3 Maple (4)
4 Greek n (2)
6 Well-informed (2)

251

Across
1 Informal speech of foreign language (3)
4 Instrument giving A to tune by (4)
6 Salmon that has just spawned (4)
7 Camellia sinensis (3)

Down
1 ___ choy; chinese cabbage (3)
2 To make good (4)
3 Japanned tinware (4)
5 Greek long e (3)

252

Across
1 Branch of learning (3)
4 Greek public ambulatory (4)
5 The bib (4)
6 Liable (3)

Down
1 On top of (4)
2 Hollow, scoop out (4)
3 E Indian hemp mat (3)
4 Health resort (3)

253

Across
1 Big lie (4)
4 Interjection of surprise (2)
5 Exists (2)
6 Inner forearm bone (4)

Down
1 Isolated pampas tree (4)
2 The Big Apple (abbr) (1,1)
3 An Indian grass (4)
5 A reflex angle (2)

254

1	2	3	4
5			
6			
7			

Across

1 Alban ___, composer (4)
5 Throughout (4)
6 Middle string of lyre (4)
7 Aspiring to aestheticism (4)

Down

1 An Anaconda (4)
2 At all, possibly (4)
3 Reserve fund (4)
4 Dry, colourless (4)

Across
1 Seemingly limitless mass (3)
4 A crack (4)
5 Eject (4)
6 A path; a ladder (3)

Down
1 Made fast (4)
2 Unconstrained (4)
3 Liable, prone (3)
4 Long lettuce (3)

256

Across
1 Sharpness of mind (4)
5 Eternity (3)
6 Auberge (3)
7 In faith, truly (4)

Down
2 Small valley (4)
3 Tam-tam (4)
4 Half-em (2)
6 Whether (2)

257

Across
1 Old wool weight (3)
4 Happen ___: meet by chance (4)
6 Hammer's end opposite face (4)
7 Hilltop, promontory (3)

Down
1 Paving rammer (3)
2 Unreserved (4)
3 A sweetheart (4)
5 Beak, bill (3)

258

Across
1 Delay (3)
4 Tailless hare (4)
5 Adjustable stop for lens (4)
6 Spent bark (3)

Down
1 Pre-euro Italian currency unit (4)
2 Of similar nature (4)
3 Something delightful (3)
4 Fruit-stone (3)

Across

1 Hebrew Q (4)
4 The Queen (abbr) (1,1)
5 Voting system (1,1)
6 Shaft of column (4)

Down

1 Punting pole (4)
2 Heraldic yellow (2)
3 To hasten (4)
5 Lodger (abbr) (1,1)

260

1	2	3	4
5			
6			
7			

Across
1 Narrow defile (4)
5 Inflatable mattress (4)
6 Thick Japanese noodles (4)
7 Impose a curfew (4)

Down
1 Go on doggedly (4)
2 Finely-meshed cotton fabric (4)
3 Deer's footprints (4)
4 Sound loudness unit (4)

261

Across

1 A craze, obsession (3)
4 Maori supernatural power (4)
5 (L) died (4)
6 To irritate (3)

Down

1 Girl, girlfriend (4)
2 The least whole number (4)
3 Opening between sandbanks (3)
4 A cat (3)

Across
1 To mark with ruddle (4)
5 Mouth-like openings (3)
6 Chess ability scale (3)
7 Coarse seaweed (4)

Down
2 The sunfish (4)
3 Theatre safety curtain (4)
4 Thank you (2)
6 ___ al: and elsewhere (2)

263

Across

1 A bone (3)
4 Incite by aid (4)
6 Wormwood leaf down (4)
7 Proposed time of leaving (abbr) (1,1,1)

Down

1 Scottish cap (3)
2 Double-reed woodwind (4)
3 Matter commented on (4)
5 A small amount (3)

264

Across
1 Serpent-like coil of feathers (3)
4 A platter (4)
5 Clever (4)
6 Hawthorn flower (3)

Down
1 Rum syrup cake (4)
2 Without others (4)
3 Ruthless cutting down (3)
4 To beat (3)

265

Across
1 Spare, extra (4)
4 Children's game (2)
5 In succession to (2)
6 Malay boat (4)

Down
1 A lame person (4)
2 ___ it: occupied in (2)
3 Australian plant genus (4)
5 Personal smell (abbr) (1,1)

266

1	2	3	4
5			
6			
7			

Across

1 White china trinkets (4)
5 The olive genus (4)
6 A scrounge (4)
7 Mythical heraldic animal (4)

Down

1 Fish with sucker ventral fin (4)
2 Jar, urn (4)
3 Phoca (4)
4 Salvia (4)

Across
1 Sibilant (3)
4 (S Afr) a grandfather (4)
5 Small cereal destructive fly (4)
6 Play the fool (3)

Down
1 A wallaroo (4)
2 Favourable slant on policy (4)
3 Underwent examination (3)
4 The start (3)

Across
1 Side of bird's head (4)
5 Nothing (3)
6 On each side (3)
7 Tree frog (4)

Down
2 Without siblings (4)
3 A runnel (4)
4 Direct from (2)
6 Expression of surprise, joy (2)

269

Across
1 (L) where (3)
4 (Scot) greedy, miserly (4)
6 Oblong cloth worn by
Arabs (4)
7 College of political science
(abbr) (1,1,1)

Down
1 Sound of disgust (3)
2 A false god (4)
3 Appearance resembling
rainbow (4)
5 In addition, likewise (3)

Across
1 Maigre (fish) (3)
4 A temple (4)
5 Slow match (4)
6 Japanese Aralia (3)

Down
1 Unit of signalling speed (4)
2 (L) in the year (4)
3 Expose to moisture (3)
4 Grippe (3)

1	**2**		**3**
4		■	
	■	**5**	
6			

Across
1 Painful (4)
4 Father (2)
5 Non-commission holders (abbr) (1,1)
6 Actual existence (4)

Down
1 Cutting tool (4)
2 About (L) (abbr) (2)
3 Time long past (4)
5 A mouth (2)

1	**2**	**3**	**4**
5			
6			
7			

Across

1 Japanese sandal (4)
5 Relating to a grandparent (4)
6 Strikebreaker (4)
7 To flog (4)

Down

1 To gamble (4)
2 King's ___, a scrofulous disease (4)
3 Terrestrial tree shrew (4)
4 An alcoholic (4)

273

Across
1 Goat's bleat (3)
4 The public purse (4)
5 Bowdlerize (4)
6 Pluto (3)

Down
1 South of France (4)
2 Unaltered (2,2)
3 A pretence (3)
4 US agent (3)

274

Across
1 Burdock (4)
5 ___ vomica, an E Indian tree (3)
6 She (3)
7 Misses the mark (4)

Down
2 Heavy blow (4)
3 Knob at base of deer's horn (4)
4 Neat (2)
6 A male (2)

275

Across

1 Long, Long ____; song by Thomas Haynes Bayly (3)
4 Theatre box (4)
6 Ale warmed and spiced (4)
7 Vietnamese lunar new year (3)

Down

1 Mountain pasture (3)
2 Taste, relish (4)
3 Ugly, cruel person (4)
5 Young sow (3)

276

Across

1 Right of holding local court (3)
4 Kingfish (4)
5 Body of Corinthian capital (4)
6 Knack of doing something (3)

Down

1 A cock fight (4)
2 Drying kiln (4)
3 ___ Sarà Sarà, what will be will be (3)
4 Female gametes (3)

277

1	2		3
4		■	
	■	5	
6			

Across
1 Indian weight (4)
4 Whether (2)
5 Bible edition (abbr) (1,1)
6 Enthusiastic about (4)

Down
1 Polynesian greenstone ornament (4)
2 From among (2)
3 Oz pm (4)
5 Position in space or time (2)

1	2	3	4
5			
6			
7			

Across
1 Prickly seed case (4)
5 Italian songs (4)
6 Wheel hub (4)
7 Character determining pitch (4)

Down
1 Judges' bench (4)
2 Russian river, mountain range (4)
3 Tear apart (4)
4 Shorten sail (4)

Across

1 Speak fondly (3)
4 Bit of paper punched out (4)
5 Demolish (building) (4)
6 Make a choice (3)

Down

1 A crack (4)
2 Drying kiln (4)
3 Poem to be sung (3)
4 ___-Magnon, early homo sapiens (3)

280

1	2	3	4
■	5		
6			■
7			

Across

1 Spumante, a sparkling wine (4)
5 Small songbird (3)
6 Knowledge (3)
7 Unrestricted (4)

Down

2 Short walk (4)
3 Fork prong (4)
4 Personal magnetism (2)
6 Stunning blow (abbr) (1,1)

Across

1 Kind (3)
4 Raised floor (4)
6 S American tree (4)
7 Horseradish tree (3)

Down

1 Auxiliary international language (3)
2 Meat (4)
3 A chilblain (4)
5 Central body in a system (3)

Across
1 Volcanic dust (3)
4 Answer to charge (4)
5 Liquor sediment (4)
6 Intense desire (3)

Down
1 On the sheltered side (4)
2 Understood (4)
3 Holds (3)
4 Work at steadily (3)

Across
1 Arched bladed cutter (4)
4 Closed (2)
5 Because in that case (2)
6 Concluding musical passage (4)

Down
1 Species of skunk (4)
2 Redecorate (2)
3 4th c BC Jewish reformer (4)
5 Take too much of drug (1,1)

1	2	3	4
5			
6			
7			

Across

1 Sola hat (4)
5 Port opposite Mull (4)
6 Fit arrow to bowstring (4)
7 Bluish-grey sticky clay (4)

Down

1 Chinese secret society (4)
2 Sixth of a drachma (4)
3 By the leave of (4)
4 Drunk (4)

285

Across
1 Cape brandy (3)
4 Chrysalis (4)
5 Corded cloth (4)
6 Scale assessing chess players (3)

Down
1 Affair of honour (4)
2 One's counterpart (4)
3 Stultifying entertainment (3)
4 (Prefix) the anterior part of (3-)

286

Across
1 Public weighing machine (4)
5 A joke; a drink (3)
6 Hail (3)
7 Series of ecological communities (4)

Down
2 Twist cotton prior to spinning (4)
3 An expert (4)
4 (Man) born (2)
6 Norse god (2)

Across

1 Projection on revolving shaft (3)

4 Of Oxford (abbr) (4)

6 Floor covering (4)

7 A saying (3)

Down

1 A defile (3)

2 Second vertebra of neck (4)

3 A W African monkey (4)

5 Since at this time (3)

Across
1 To a ___: exactly (3)
4 A mixture; a crowd (4)
5 Excitedly eager (4)
6 A choice marble (3)

Down
1 Roman garment (4)
2 (Scot) a moment ago (4)
3 Urge on (3)
4 Web of rope-yarn (3)

Across
1 Scale of mineral hardness (4)
4 Batting (2)
5 German joint stock company (abbr) (2)
6 Ponte Vecchio river (4)

Down
1 A rock-forming mineral (4)
2 Practicable (2)
3 Nutritive palm pith (4)
5 If (2)

290

1	2	3	4
5			
6			
7			

Across
1 German count (4)
5 Confidential assistant (4)
6 Covered colonnade (4)
7 Something destructive (4)

Down
1 Breathe in sharply (4)
2 A liturgy (4)
3 Troubles (4)
4 An exploit (4)

291

Across
1 Music similar to reggae (3)
4 Naval hail (4)
5 Heraldic animal (4)
6 Greek letter written P (3)

Down
1 King of Persia (4)
2 Serbian folk dance (4)
3 Affirmative vote (3)
4 Scottish river, town at its mouth (3)

292

Across
1 Beast's foreleg (4)
5 Long narrow spade (3)
6 Chess proficiency scale (3)
7 Story with a veiled meaning (4)

Down
2 Join, as by marriage (4)
3 Administrative assembly (4)
4 In succession to (2)
6 ___ dash; punctuation mark (2)

Across

1 Former French coin (3)
4 A mere trifle (4)
6 Plant of the mallow family (4)
7 Type of vassal's tenure (3)

Down

1 Female suffix (-3)
2 Head covering (4)
3 (Heraldry) wavy (4)
5 Nazi political district (3)

294

Across
1 Chilling (3)
4 Without another (4)
5 Son of Judah (4)
6 School of whales (3)

Down
1 Inner Hebridean island (4)
2 A gripping instrument (4)
3 Intense urge (3)
4 Soft wet place (3)

Across
1 Elderly (4)
4 Japanese drama (2)
5 (Mus) forced (abbr) (2)
6 Hilarious performance (4)

Down
1 Ansate cross (4)
2 Turn (2)
3 Dexterous (4)
5 Accordingly (2)

1	2	3	4
5			
6			
7			

Across
1 (Scot) livid (4)
5 Indian camel (4)
6 A lepton (4)
7 16th of a rupee (4)

Down
1 Anaconda (4)
2 Calm, quiet (Scot) (4)
3 Soon (4)
4 Liquid heating vessel (4)

Across
1 Chance (3)
4 Irish clan (4)
5 Measure of surface size (4)
6 Ninth man in boat (3)

Down
1 Principal male (4)
2 Culminating point (4)
3 Former Spanish currency (abbr) (3)
4 Bag-like structure (3)

298

Across

1 Small wood (4)
5 A crude rubber (3)
6 Past (3)
7 Soft, timid person (4)

Down

2 French novelist (4)
3 (Indian) potato (4)
4 Editorial I (2)
6 Kame (2)

Across
1 100 sq m (3)
4 Safe burglar (4)
6 Keenness (4)
7 Tinge (3)

Down
1 Indeed (3)
2 Salmon nesting place (4)
3 Having just laid (4)
5 Move horse to right (3)

300

Across
1 Raise aloft (3)
4 Black (4)
5 Otter's den (4)
6 Self-confidence (3)

Down
1 Hit hard (4)
2 Serbian folk dance (4)
3 In addition (3)
4 A female (3)

301

Across
1 Excitedly eager (4)
4 A beloved (2)
5 Sacred intoned syllable (2)
6 To tirl (4)

Down
1 Part-open (4)
2 To fare (2)
3 Yarn with hard core (4)
5 A mouth (2)

302

Across
1 Launce (4)
5 American ____: agave (4)
6 Gloomy (4)
7 Without (4)

Down
1 Steals (4)
2 In the style of (4)
3 A substantive (4)
4 À sieve, strainer (4)

303

Across
1 Alias (abbr) (1,1,1)
4 Wiry grass (4)
5 Greek cupid (4)
6 A lout (3)

Down
1 Relating to flying (4)
2 Small group of wildfowl (4)
3 Precursor of the WRAC (1,1,1)
4 Turkish governor (3)

304

Across
1 Dexterous (4)
5 Winglike bone process (3)
6 A unit (3)
7 African nut tree (4)

Down
2 Per person (4)
3 Leave hurriedly (4)
4 Volunteer servicemen (abbr) (1,1)
6 Norse god (2)

305

Across
1 Play, sing twice (3)
4 Species with environmental characteristics (4)
6 Short, narrow lane (4)
7 Bill (3)

Down
1 Noise measure (3)
2 A symbol (4)
3 Fermented rice drink (4)
5 Young woman entering society (3)

306

Across
1 Tepid (3)
4 Small shark (4)
5 Related (4)
6 Involuntary habitual response (3)

Down
1 Evil Norse god (4)
2 Impressive, large scale (4)
3 The Great ___: London (3)
4 To flog (3)

Across
1 Voting system (abbr) (1,1,1,1)
4 Fourth note of scale (2)
5 Interjection calling attention (2)
6 Ship's small boat (4)

Down
1 White person (black slang) (4)
2 ___ non troppo: but not too much (2)
3 Doff in salutation (4)
5 Cry of pain (2)

308

Across
1 Fail to answer question in quiz (4)
5 (S Afr) a grandmother (4)
6 Solid line of hot type (4)
7 Pacific plant with edible rootstock (4)

Down
1 Stake in a game (4)
2 (L) a hall (4)
3 Fine misty rain (4)
4 Nutritive pith substance (4)

Across
1 Died without issue (L) (abbr) (3)
4 Shivering fit (4)
5 French policeman (4)
6 Spread grass to dry (3)

Down
1 Eye impertinently (4)
2 Member of pig family (4)
3 Chest muscle (3)
4 Sternward (3)

310

1	2	3	4
	5		
6			
7			

Across
1 Elongated cells (4)
5 Pretentious odds and ends (3)
6 Scull (3)
7 Ptarmigan (4)

Down
2 A check, restraint (4)
3 Nag about trivialities (4)
4 Novel by Stephen King (2)
6 Those not holding commission (abbr) (1,1)

Across
1 School of whales (3)
4 Got off vehicle (4)
6 Soya bean paste (4)
7 Hybrid Himalaya cattle (3)

Down
1 Jack of clubs (loo) (3)
2 Rank smelling (4)
3 Algerian reedy grass (4)
5 Overly (3)

Across

1 Suitable (3)
4 Heavy Roman javelins (4)
5 Enough (4)
6 (Animals) offspring (3)

Down

1 (Fr) elder, senior (4)
2 Burn, scald (4)
3 Prepare skins for white leather (3)
4 A turtle harpoon (3)

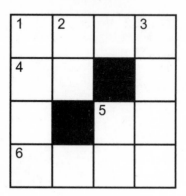

Across
1 Lean upon (4)
4 A silk (abbr) (1,1)
5 Derived from (2)
6 A taller Japanese people, language (4)

Down
1 ___ Tofana, a secret poison (4)
2 A Canadian province (abbr) (1,1)
3 Soy bean curd (4)
5 At the risk of (2)

314

Across
1 Take on board (4)
5 Unproductive (4)
6 Square doorway pilaster (4)
7 An equipage (4)

Down
1 Shellfish larva (4)
2 Sharpen on smooth stone (4)
3 Jot (4)
4 A fishing-boat (4)

315

Across
1 Semiconductor device (abbr) (1,1,1)
4 The south of France (4)
5 CGS work units (4)
6 Tea (3)

Down
1 100 kurus (4)
2 Nervous (4)
3 Treat with contempt (3)
4 Encountered (3)

316

Across

1 Pakistan language (4)
5 A way of escape (3)
6 A native American (3)
7 Riches (4)

Down

2 Medieval stringed instrument (4)
3 Single combat to decide quarrel (4)
4 (L) as (2)
6 Mounted (2)

317

Across
1 Reserve (3)
4 Slip of metal to adjust gap (4)
6 'Sea' on the moon, Mars (4)
7 Fixed bench in church (3)

Down
1 Distinctive doctrine (3)
2 Crack in the skin (4)
3 Ireland (4)
5 A gull (3)

318

Across
1 Slighted feeling (3)
4 Volcanic material (4)
5 Soon (4)
6 A radio-navigation system (3)

Down
1 Rectangular compartment (4)
2 Cry of Bacchic frenzy (4)
3 Spent bark (3)
4 A falling behind (3)

319

Across
1 Indigo (4)
4 A success (2)
5 God willing (L) (abbr) (1,1)
6 Unrestrained celebration (4)

Down
1 Money-changing (4)
2 Japanese drama (2)
3 Begin to wage (4)
5 By the grace of God (L) (abbr) (1,1)

320

1	2	3	4
5			
6			
7			

Across
1 Hurdle barrier on racecourse (4)
5 Air (It) (4)
6 Hound's pendulous upper lip (4)
7 The Volunteer state (abbr) (4)

Down
1 Weak-minded (4)
2 Border within shield (4)
3 The spleen (4)
4 Fine cambric (4)

321

Across
1 Plant of mulberry family (3)
4 Maori war dance (4)
5 Sins (4)
6 Roe of salmon (3)

Down
1 Hasten (4)
2 Gumbo (4)
3 Ballet step, dance (3)
4 Fashionably informed (3)

322

Across
1 Bush of matted hair over brow (4)
5 Fish of carp family (3)
6 Japanese species of Aralia (3)
7 The sunfish (4)

Down
2 Bathing beach (4)
3 False notion (4)
4 Remain without change (2)
6 ___ and ah: hesitate (2)

323

Across
1 She-antelope (3)
4 Clever (4)
6 Film, membrane (4)
7 Sweet potato (3)

Down
1 (India) mail (3)
2 Act as directed (4)
3 (It) She (4)
5 Timber tree (3)

324

Across

1 Mark aimed at in curling (3)
4 Spoken exam (4)
5 All others (4)
6 Whimsical (3)

Down

1 A gallows (4)
2 In plentiful supply (4)
3 Aircraft distress radio beacon (1,1,1)
4 Viral infection of sheep (3)

325

Across
1 (Poetic) in a thirsty state (4)
4 2 Down: Commotion (2-2)
5 Pica measure (2)
6 Wrack (4)

Down
1 Species of skunk (4)
2 See 4 Across
3 Trek carrying heavy equipment (4)
5 Elevated railroad (2)

326

1	2	3	4
5			
6			
7			

Across

1 Bits punched out of paper tape (4)

5 ____ lamp, with bright viscous shape changes (4)

6 Smart ____, a would-be clever person (4)

7 Long ago (4)

Down

1 The human body (4)

2 Ring round the moon (4)

3 Allege in a legal pleading (4)

4 Small river fish (4)

327

Across
1 Scots 'do' (3)
4 A roll of parchment (4)
5 Fail to use (4)
6 Marriage portion (3)

Down
1 Public expression of feeling (4)
2 Dismounted (4)
3 English language teaching (1,1,1)
4 A silk cocoon (3)

Across
1 Risky (4)
5 Sheltered (3)
6 House, farm in south of France (3)
7 (Archaic) to (4)

Down
2 Blank metal disc in coin-making (4)
3 A party, gathering (4)
4 You (2)
6 Greek M (2)

Across
1 Pair of variety artists (3)
4 An entrance; a reveal (4)
6 Of variegated colours (4)
7 Spread cut grass to dry (3)

Down
1 To mortgage, pawn (3)
2 Least whole number (4)
3 S-moulding (4)
5 Standing apart (3)

330

Across
1 The winning of five tricks (3)
4 Body of legend on a subject (4)
5 (Australia) cricket, football ground (4)
6 By means of (3)

Down
1 Wheel hub (4)
2 Seaweed jelly (4)
3 Colour-television system (acronym) (1,1,1)
4 To steep in alcohol (3)

331

Across
1 Rounds (abbr) (4)
4 (US) male address (2)
5 Thereupon (2)
6 Drawn, paint (4)

Down
1 First fratricide victim (4)
2 Missouri (abbr) (2)
3 Of Oxford (abbr) (4)
5 NCO (abbr) (1,1)

Across

1 Toothless, tailless amphibian (4)
5 In a proficient manner (4)
6 Muslim market-place (4)
7 Powdered (4)

Down

1 A drinking cup (4)
2 Cor anglais (4)
3 Chemical compound (4)
4 Earth dug out and thrown up (4)

333

Across
1 Big bell (3)
4 Quaintly pleasing (4)
5 Death anniversary (4)
6 Pouch (3)

Down
1 Bombardon (4)
2 Of the ear (4)
3 Satisfied (3)
4 Long lettuce (3)

334

Across
1 Must (grape juice) (4)
5 Gone, since (3)
6 Sesame (3)
7 Mixture, medley (4)

Down
2 Stem of a note (4)
3 Grapefruit cross (4)
4 Way of working (abbr) (1,1)
6 Until (2)

335

Across
1 Witty saying (3)
4 Lowest small intestinal parts (4)
6 Heather (4)
7 Marked area on billiard table (3)

Down
1 Wire diameter measure (3)
2 Smelling rank (4)
3 (Arch) injury, affliction (4)
5 A generation (3)

336

Across
1 To be played twice (3)
4 Unwilling (4)
5 A duck (4)
6 Obsolete Indian coin (3)

Down
1 Fenced enclosure in Africa (4)
2 Two in a relationship (4)
3 Feminine (3)
4 Schizophrenic condition (abbr) (1,1,1)

337

Across
1 Street urchin (4)
4 (Egyp) soul of dead person (2)
5 Consumption (abbr) (1,1)
6 European commerce organisation (abbr) (1,1,1,1)

Down
1 Small African tree, edible fruit (4)
2 Egyptian sun-god (2)
3 Cake soaked in rum syrup (4)
5 Manx race (abbr) (1,1)

338

¹	²	³	⁴
⁵			
⁶			
⁷			

Across
1 Celebrity (4)
5 Group forming subdivision (4)
6 Fool, idiot (4)
7 Draw together (4)

Down
1 Strong, unpleasant smell (4)
2 Expression of failure to understand (4)
3 Small car (4)
4 (Fr) state, rank (4)

339

Across
1 Parastic maggot in horses (3)
4 (Obs) a buffoon (4)
5 Olive genus (4)
6 Rocky height (3)

Down
1 Long, sweeping uppercut (4)
2 Hebrew dry measure (4)
3 Infused drink (3)
4 Pithy saying (3)

Across
1 Newts (4)
5 Odd, droll (3)
6 Jack of clubs (loo) (3)
7 Amazon basin people (4)

Down
2 German wife (4)
3 Make a mound around (4)
4 Senior NCO (abbr) (1,1)
6 Gym (abbr) (1,1)

341

Across
1 Young sow (3)
4 Vertical slit in castle wall (4)
6 Small reef island in S Pacific (4)
7 (Scot) carrion (3)

Down
1 Timber tree (3)
2 Appearance (4)
3 Carry burden (4)
5 To impose (3)

342

Across
1 Ace of trumps in gleek (3)
4 Sikh steel bangle (4)
5 Symbol, image (4)
6 (Mus) held (abbr) (3)

Down
1 Be silent! (4)
2 Pistol (4)
3 A curse (3)
4 Small pocket violin (3)

343

1	2		3
4		■	
	■	5	
6			

Across
1 A bullock (4)
4 Chamber (2)
5 Atomic mass unit (2)
6 Foolish or eccentric person (4)

Down
1 Fat, bacon (4)
2 Near (2)
3 Hard, durable wood (4)
5 Impersonate (2)

344

Across
1 Antarctic NZ dependency (4)
5 Kingfish (4)
6 Croatia currency unit (4)
7 Insulated container for cool drinks (4)

Down
1 Light rain, mist (4)
2 ___ musivum: mosaic (4)
3 Collapsed (4)
4 Chaise (4)

345

Across
1 Hebrew marginal Bible reading (1'2)
4 Enclosure for beasts (4)
5 Duck such as pochard (4)
6 Water barrier (3)

Down
1 (Hindu) earthly desire (4)
2 A rawhide thong (4)
3 Keen resentment (3)
4 Hallucinatory substance (abbr) (1,1,1)

346

Across
1 The dogfish (4)
5 Greek letter printed P (3)
6 A promontory (3)
7 Afresh (4)

Down
2 (Slang) pistol (4)
3 Clarified butter (4)
4 A turn (2)
6 In this year (L) (abbr) (1,1)

347

Across
1 Cobra de capello (3)
4 Member of pig family (4)
6 Indian weight (4)
7 To annoy (3)

Down
1 A fool (3)
2 Solid fatty tissue (4)
3 Arch support (4)
5 Unbuttered (3)

348

Across
1 Catholic dignitary (3)
4 Botswana currency unit (4)
5 Impressive, large-scale (4)
6 Unruly 50s adolescent (3)

Down
1 To trick (4)
2 Rank-smelling (4)
3 Waterproof coat (3)
4 Slighted feeling (3)

349

Across

1 Legal rights (4)
4 Dieu ___ mon droit (2)
5 (Scot) very, same (2)
6 (Heraldry) horizontal band (4)

Down

1 (Circus) a rope (4)
2 Doh, formerly (2)
3 A long time (4)
5 Roman 12-ounce pound (2)

350

1	2	3	4
5			
6			
7			

Across
1 Attar (4)
5 Saharan shifting sand dune areas (4)
6 Diseased lung rattle (4)
7 Team of oxen (4)

Down
1 Sculls (4)
2 (Mining) a fault (4)
3 Web (4)
4 Kibbutz melon variety (4)

Across
1 Mark aimed at in curling (3)
4 Wagon awning (4)
5 Native child's nurse (4)
6 The low-down (3)

Down
1 Prison sentence (4)
2 Impetuosity (4)
3 Barred D (3)
4 Tip of animal's tail (3)

352

1	2	3	4
■	5		
6			■
7			

Across
1 Seaweed (4)
5 High tone (3)
6 Language developed from Esperanto (3)
7 A literal (4)

Down
2 Mistress of a house (4)
3 Semi-liquid substance (4)
4 Monetary unit of Laos (2)
6 Sweet vermouth (abbr) (2)

353

Across
1 Sovereignty (3)
4 Harsh, grating (4)
6 (Prefix) middle (4-)
7 Fling (3)

Down
1 Encircling band (3)
2 Son of Zeus and Hera (4)
3 To ridicule (4)
5 (Spencer) to vex (3)

Across

1 Viper (3)
4 Darts player's line (4)
5 (Obs) pierce (4)
6 Spread new-mown grass (3)

Down

1 Approx: 0.4 ha (4)
2 Fitted with shoes (4)
3 A cricket stump (3)
4 Make a choice (3)

¹	²		³
⁴		■	
	■	⁵	
⁶			

Across
1 A hairstyle (4)
4 American chopper (2)
5, 6 (L) entirely (2,4)

Down
1 Sell by auction (4)
2 Steer (2)
3 Dry sherry (4)
5 Personal magnetism (2)

1	2	3	4
5			
6			
7			

Across
1 Fine, excellent (4)
5 Turkish spirit (4)
6 Big lie (4)
7 S-curve (4)

Down
1 (Scot) call to horse to stop (4)
2 Principle of connection (4)
3 Fruit used in Caribbean cookery (4)
4 Apparel (4)

357

Across

1 Schoolmaster (3)
4 Ponder (4)
5 Standing concert (4)
6 1/100 yen (3)

Down

1 Aggrieved (4)
2 Strength (4)
3 Type of sleep (abbr) (1,1,1)
4 Second postscript (abbr) (1,1,1)

358

Across
1 (It) look there (4)
5 Faint-hearted person (3)
6 Arab stringed instrument (3)
7 Fish pond (4)

Down
2 Expression of impatience (4)
3 Give way (4)
4 Subject to (2)
6 Osmium symbol (2)

359

Across
1 Hasten (3)
4 Official proceedings (4)
6 Relish (4)
7 Obsolete nigh (3)

Down
1 Eel-like marine vertebrate (3)
2 Picture symbol (4)
3 Case of sewing articles (4)
5 Chewed (3)

360

Across
1 Moke (3)
4 Rounds (abbr) (4)
5 Hard, black (4)
6 Soak (3)

Down
1 Early pulpit (4)
2 Smoky obscurity (4)
3 A disciple (3)
4 ___ alienum (L): a debt (3)

361

1	2		3
4		■	
	■	5	
6			

Across
1 Moiety (4)
4 The ne plus ultra (2)
5 Greek M (2)
6 Charon's river (4)

Down
1 Express disapproval (4)
2 Monetary unit of Laos (2)
3 State of flow (4)
5 Expression of surprise (2)

362

Across
1 Glance over quickly (4)
5 Instrument bow (4)
6 Shinto lord (4)
7 Wide-spouted jug (4)

Down
1 Fermented rice drink (4)
2 Fowl's crop (4)
3 Culmination in career (4)
4 Film ___, 1940s, 50s style (4)

363

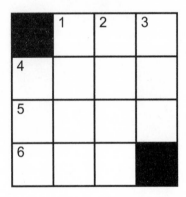

Across
1 Brother, friar (3)
4 Tongue of land between rivers (4)
5 Discover unexpectedly (4)
6 Human potential-raising programme (3)

Down
1 Ditch, moat (4)
2 Entranced (4)
3 (Arch) pay the penalty for (3)
4 Billiard table area (3)

364

Across
1 (Heraldry) sheaf of wheat (4)
5 Doomed soon to die (3)
6 Frequently (3)
7 Cloth colourist (4)

Down
2 (Obs) to trust (4)
3 Anatomical network (4)
4 Multiplied into (2)
6 Reichenbach's force name (2)

365

Across

1 ____ scanner: 3-D X-ray machine (3)
4 Follow slavishly (4)
6 (Woman) sexy (4)
7 Hospital department (abbr) (1,1,1)

Down

1 Edible mushroom (3)
2 Long for (4)
3 Except, other ____ (4)
5 Excessive (abbr) (1,1,1)

366

Across
1 Metric land measure (3)
4 Flat area, region (4)
5 Mountain used by the Aloadae (4)
6 To kill (3)

Down
1 Further (4)
2 Scrape, as a fiddle (4)
3 Basque Homeland and Freedom (3)
4 Cup, trophy (3)

Across

1 Edge, border, as of the sun (4)
4 In continuance (2)
5 Pulp's 1983 album (2)
6 Snipe-like shore bird (4)

Down

1 Appearance (4)
2 Wearing (2)
3 Place where two edges meet (4)
5 Cry of joy (2)

1	2	3	4
5			
6			
7			

Across
1 Chinese ounce (4)
5 Mid-19c shade attached to lady's hat (4)
6 Stone chest tomb (4)
7 Bird's joint corresponding to ankle (4)

Down
1 Stitched-down fold (4)
2 Against (4)
3 Beside (4)
4 Little (4)

369

Across
1 An udder (3)
4 Fabric with highly glazed finish (4)
5 Robbery 'take' (4)
6 Distinctive doctrine (3)

Down
1 Prejudice (4)
2 Wake-robin (4)
3 Preparation for the hair (3)
4 Greek letter printed X (3)

370

Across
1 Worthless things (4)
5 Image of self (3)
6 Room in harem (3)
7 (Obs) a buffoon (4)

Down
2 Decorate room again (4)
3 Ancient alphabet (4)
4 In contact with (2)
6 Sacred, intoned syllable (2)

371

Across
1 Watch pocket (3)
4 Sacred Egyptian bird (4)
6 Lacquered tinware (4)
7 Add to (3)

Down
1 A canto, division of poem (3)
2 Hautboy (4)
3 To cheat (4)
5 Diocese (3)

372

Across
1 ___ culpa: I am to blame (3)
4 Sit upright (4)
5 Bones (4)
6 To a ___: exactly (3)

Down
1 Middle string of lyre (4)
2 Irish Gaelic (4)
3 Alias (abbr) (1,1,1)
4 Accumulated pool of bets (3)

Across
1 French priest (4)
4 ___ facto: actual (2)
5 By way of (2)
6 Unconstrained manner (4)

Down
1 Cutting tool (4)
2 Take place (2)
3 Sea-eagle (4)
5 Iceland (IVR) (2)

374

1	2	3	4
5			
6			
7			

Across
1 Hindu eclipse demon (4)
5 Greek war god (4)
6 Collection of data (4)
7 A sieve (4)

Down
1 Heap, large number (4)
2 Operatic songs (It) (4)
3 Steering apparatus (4)
4 Advantageous purposes (4)

375

Across
1 Jack of clubs (loo) (3)
4 Sporting occasion (4)
5 Graphic display symbol (4)
6 Born (fem) (3)

Down
1 By the leave of (4)
2 ___ vera, cosmetic juice (4)
3 Provide crew (3)
4 Snare (3)

376

1	2	3	4
	5		
6			
7			

Across
1 Dolichotis (4)
5 Shovel for resting ore (3)
6 Horseradish tree (3)
7 Kames (4)

Down
2 Birds (4)
3 A Rajput prince (4)
4 (Archaic) if (2)
6 Ancient Egyptian soul (2)

Across
1 Bitter vetch (3)
4 Stop short (4)
6 Soft white cheese (4)
7 Ready to learn (3)

Down
1 Sink, decline (3)
2 Cheerleader's skirt (2-2)
3 Creamy paste of clay and water (4)
5 (Scot) matted wool (3)

378

Across

1 Renegade (3)
4 Refuse left after wine making (4)
5 Spanish motorcycle manufacturer (4)
6 Dagoba finial (3)

Down

1 Lay building flat to ground (4)
2 East end of church choir (4)
3 Infused beverage (3)
4 Balderdash (3)

379

Across
1 An instant (4)
4 Bone (2)
5 ___ tree: the pipal (2)
6 To incline (4)

Down
1 To tease (4)
2 Exists (2)
3 Fruit purée (4)
5 Happen (2)

380

1	2	3	4
5			
6			
7			

Across
1 Dead (4)
5 Of a grandparent (4)
6 Wormwood leaf down (4)
7 Interjection 'I don't understand' (4)

Down
1 Monk in Tibet (4)
2 Eden its 1st Earl (4)
3 Biological categories (4)
4 Vigour and style (4)

Across

1 Set in contrast (abbr) (3)
4 Indian plant of madder family (4)
5 Cameo agate (4)
6 Aye (3)

Down

1 Lied ____ worte: song without words (4)
2 Les ____ Bas: the Netherlands (4)
3 Host box (3)
4 Affectedly shy (3)

382

Across
1 Damask rose essence (4)
5 A smart blow (3)
6 1/100 yen (3)
7 In faith, truly (4)

Down
2 Affectedly pretty (4)
3 Coarse seaweed (4)
4 ___ art, giving illusion of movement (2)
6 (Mus) with sudden emphasis (abbr) (2)

Across

1 Form of equitable ownership (3)
4 Tell tales (4)
6 A jot (4)
7 Ability to perceive without normal senses (abbr) (1,1,1)

Down

1 ____ supra: where mentioned above (3)
2 Blackthorn fruit (4)
3 Corrodes (4)
5 Breakfast roll (3)

Across
1 Drain the energy from (3)
4 Membranous flap (4)
5 Seed appendage (4)
6 One behaving dishonourably (3)

Down
1 N American short-billed rail (4)
2 Among (4)
3 Colour-TV system (abbr) (1,1,1)
4 Shellac resin (3)

385

Across

1 Three-handed card game (4)
4 (L) in this year (abbr) (1,1)
5 'It' (abbr) (1,1)
6 In a frenzy (4)

Down

1 A branch of Islam (4)
2 (Scot) jackdaw (2)
3 Hard wood (4)
5 Likewise (2)

386

1	**2**	**3**	**4**
5			
6			
7			

Across
1 Anguillidae (4)
5 Graf ____, German WW2 battleship (4)
6 ___-Pei, muscular Chinese dog (4)
7 Move gently (4)

Down
1 (Ger) chimney-hood (4)
2 Hebrew dry goods measure (4)
3 Yarn measures (4)
4 Series of ecological communities (4)

387

Across
1 An honour (abbr) (1,1,1)
4 A lesson (4)
5 Time periods (4)
6 Pike-like fish (3)

Down
1 Very good, great (4)
2 Wooden stand for carrying the dead (4)
3 Bitter vetch (3)
4 Steal, carry off (3)

388

1	2	3	4
	5		
6			
7			

Across

1 The world of phenomena (4)
5 An effective restraint (3)
6 Fruit-stone (3)
7 Linked pair (4)

Down

2 Got off vehicle (4)
3 The yellowhammer (4)
4 (L) before the day (abbr) (1,1)
6 Obtrusively religious (2)

389

1	2	3	
4			5
6			
	7		

Across
1 Panaji its capital (3)
4 Isolated pampas tree (4)
6 Unit of signalling speed (4)
7 Scottish National Trust (abbr) (1,1,1)

Down
1 US Navy sailor (3)
2 Arabian country (4)
3 To border (4)
5 God's (in oaths) (3)

390

Across
1 The start (3)
4 Stare impertinently (4)
5 A threepenny-bit (4)
6 To work up (3)

Down
1 Fearsome person (4)
2 Bloodhound's upper lip (4)
3 Tarboosh (3)
4 Excessive (abbr) (1,1,1)

391

Across

1 Young sow (4)

4,2D Up to some criminal activity (2,2)

5 Applied to (2)

6 (Hindu) the first mortal (4)

Down

1 High (venison etc.) (4)

2 See 4 Across

3 Indian police station (4)

5 British honour (abbr) (1,1)

392

1	2	3	4
5			
6			
7			

Across

1 Riches (4)
5 Case for sewing articles (4)
6 A NZ bracken (4)
7 (L) let it stand (4)

Down

1 Pampers (4)
2 (Fr) state, rank (4)
3 Bronze Age trumpet (4)
4 Formal command (4)

393

Across

1 Type of petroleum (abbr) (1,1,1)
4 Chinese monetary unit (4)
5 An impulse (4)
6 Dirt-clotted wool tuft on sheep (3)

Down

1 Former Italian currency unit (4)
2 Large, rough slate (4)
3 'The Raven' poet (3)
4 Mass of coal holed or undercut (3)

394

Across
1 White paint for the face (4)
5 Drowned valley (3)
6 A decline (3)
7 To flirt (4)

Down
2 Central Asian wheeled carriage (4)
3 Strengthening bars (4)
4 Swedish locomotive series (2)
6 Print space (2)

Across

1 Waterproof coat (3)
4 Tick over (4)
6 Monetary unit of Cambodia (4)
7 Deuce (3)

Down

1 Russian farming commune (3)
2 Passage into mine (4)
3 Lower corner of sail (4)
5 Chess skill scale (3)

396

Across
1 Form of Jamaican music (3)
4 Fatuous person (4)
5 Slight mention (4)
6 Type (3)

Down
1 Feed livestock on cut green grass (4)
2 Fail, break down (out) (4)
3 Fitting (3)
4 Clarified butter (3)

Across
1 Light aeroplane (4)
4 Fashionable (2)
5 Value expressing degree of acidity (1,1)
6 Vocal solo (4)

Down
1 Glass substitute (4)
2 Just after (2)
3 Ditch containing fence (2-2)
5 Private eye (abbr) (1,1)

398

1	2	3	4
5			
6			
7			

Across
1 Street acceptability (4)
5 Liquor of a tan vat (4)
6 In law, a delay (4)
7 Jewish month (4)

Down
1 Stupor (4)
2 Crucifix (4)
3 5th or 4th century BC Jewish priest (4)
4 Kind, lovable person (4)

399

Across
1 The Mosaic code (3)
4 Opening where ducts enter organs (4)
5 Single thing, person (4)
6 Have the better of (3)

Down
1 Flax (4)
2 Perched, settled (4)
3 Thai Buddhist temple (3)
4 Keep close to (3)

400

Across

1 Indian large cylindrical drum (4)
5 Mouthlike openings (3)
6 A grape (3)
7 Money (4)

Down

2 (Naut) hauled, raised up (4)
3 Viva voce (4)
4 Lo! (2)
6 Riding, on horseback (2)

SOLUTIONS

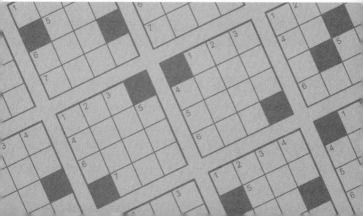

Solutions

Across
1 Vail. **4** Ob. **5** sa. **6** Koff.

Down
1 Volk. **2** AB. **3** Loaf. **5** Sf.

Across
1 Pawn. **5** Ogre. **6** Rear. **7** Neck.

Down
1 Porn. **2** Agee. **3** WRAC. **4** Nerk.

Across
1 All. **4** Floe. **5** Olid. **6** Par.

Down
1 Alla. **2** Loir. **3** Led. **4** Fop.

Solutions

Across
1 Acre. **5** Haw. **6** Nag. **7** Orgy.

Down
2 Char. **3** Ragg. **4** EW. **6** No.

4

Across
1 Sea. **4** Ipso. **6** Chin. **7** -ase.

Down
1 Sic. **2** Epha. **3** As is. **5** One.

5

Across
1 Can. **4** Hele. **5** Ergo. **6** Lea.

Down
1 Cere. **2** Alga. **3** Neo. **4** Hel.

6

Solutions

7

Across
1 Suit. **4** TT. **5** Jo. **6** Mean.

Down
1 Stum. **2** Ut. **3** Tron. **5** Ja.

8

Across
1 Fess. **5** Eale. **6** Trip. **7** Ants.

Down
1 Feta. **2** Earn. **3** Slit. **4** Seps.

9

Across
1 Fap. **4** Blue. **5** Aunt. **6** Tee.

Down
1 Flue. **2** Aune. **3** Pet. **4** Bat.

Solutions

Across
1 Icky. **5** Oat. **6** Ask. **7** Shan.

Down
2 Cosh. **3** Kaka. **4** Yt. **6** As.

10

Across
1 Arc. **4** Lerp. **6** Tier. **7** Sey.

Down
1 Alt. **2** Reis. **3** Cree. **5** Pry.

11

Across
1 NCO. **4** Woof. **5** Adit. **6** Yet.

Down
1 Node. **2** Coit. **3** Oft. **4** Way.

12

Solutions

13

Across
1 Amok. **4** Xu. **5** AK. **6** Simi.

Down
1 Axis. **2** Mu. **3** Kaki. **5** AM.

14

Across
1 Test. **5** Uxor. **6** Tori. **7** Undo.

Down
1 Tutu. **2** Exon. **3** Sord. **4** Trio.

15

Across
1 Ion. **4** Arba. **5** Goon. **6** Ens.

Down
1 Iron. **2** Obos. **3** Nan. **4** Age.

Solutions

Across
1 Naga. **5** May. **6** Sim. **7** Oryx.

Down
2 Amir. **3** Gamy. **4** Ay. **6** So.

16

Across
1 Col. **4** Avid. **6** Dame. **7** LBW.

Down
1 Cad. **2** Oval. **3** Limb. **5** Dew.

17

Across
1 Las. **4** Jink. **5** Inky. **6** Noh.

Down
1 Lino. **2** Ankh. **3** Sky. **4** Jin.

18

Solutions

19

Across
1 Sorb. 4 CD. 5 Bi. 6 Yo-yo.

Down
1 Scry. 2 Od. 3 Brio. 5 By.

20

Across
1 Stud. 5 Ohio. 6 Soss. 7 Outs.

Down
1 So-So. 2 Thou. 3 Uist. 4 Doss.

21

Across
1 Lek. 4 Saxe. 5 Ropy. 6 Iso.

Down
1 Laos. 2 Expo. 3 Key. 4 Sri.

Solutions

Across
1 Mast. **5** Bio. **6** Cep. **7** Alec.

Down
2 Abel. **3** Sipe. **4** To. **6** Ca.

22

Across
1 A la. **4** Nile. **6** Doob. **7** Neb.

Down
1 And. **2** Lion. **3** Aloe. **5** Ebb.

23

Across
1 Bot. **4** Sego. **5** Peat. **6** Arm.

Down
1 Beer. **2** Ogam. **3** Tot. **4** Spa.

24

Solutions

25

Across
1 Ogee. 4 Yu. 5 Ur-. 6 Rama.

Down
1 Oyer. 2 Gu. 3 Ezra. 5 Um.

26

Across
1 Parr. 5 Anoa. 6 Risp. 7 Plat.

Down
1 Parp. 2 Anil. 3 Rosa. 4 Rapt.

27

Across
1 Cru. 4 Pout. 5 Else. 6 Gee.

Down
1 Cole. 2 Ruse. 3 Ute. 4 Peg.

Solutions

Across
1 Wasm. **5** Loo. **6** E'er. **7** Debt.

Down
2 Alee. **3** Sorb. **4** Mo. **6** Ed.

28

Across
1 Set. **4** Obol. **6** Pome. **7** Rex.

Down
1 Sop. **2** Ebor. **3** Tome. **5** Lex.

29

Across
1 Rob. **4** Aero-. **5** Prex. **6** Teg.

Down
1 Rere. **2** Oreg. **3** Box. **4** Apt.

30

Solutions

31

Across
1 Swab. **4** He. **5** OR. **6** Duff.

Down
1 Shad. **2** We. **3** Barf. **5** Of.

32

Across
1 Toga. **5** Star. **6** Atom. **7** Roly.

Down
1 Tsar. **2** Otto. **3** Gaol. **4** Army.

33

Across
1 Gee. **4** Sain. **5** Oils. **6** Gad.

Down
1 Gaia. **2** Eild. **3** Ens. **4** Sog.

Solutions

Across
1 Fard. **5** Hoo. **6** Zek. **7** Omen.

Down
2 Ahem. **3** Roke. **4** Do. **6** Zo.

34

Across
1 Twy-. **4** Whoa. **6** Pern. **7** Tea.

Down
1 Twp. **2** Whet. **3** Yore. **5** Ana.

35

Across
1 Tau. **4** Swig. **5** Kith. **6** ITU.

Down
1 Twit. **2** Aitu. **3** Ugh. **4** Ski.

36

Solutions

37

Across
1 Scag. 4 Ka. 5 Of. 6 Punt.

Down
1 Skip. 2 Ca. 3 Gift. 5 On.

38

Across
1 Cosi. 5 Arks. 6 Glum. 7 Eyas.

Down
1 Cage. 2 Orly. 3 Skua. 4 Isms.

39

Across
1 Kye. 4 Sear. 5 Ance. 6 Yok.

Down
1 Keno. 2 Yack. 3 Ere. 4 Say.

Solutions

Across
1 Jess. **5** Sar. **6** Bam. **7** Yuan.

Down
2 Esau. **3** Sama. **4** sr. **6** By.

40

Across
1 Sac. **4** Erat. **6** Nide. **7** Dew.

Down
1 Sen. **2** Arid. **3** Cade. **5** Tew.

41

Across
1 Inn. **4** Snog. **5** Orca. **6** Lek.

Down
1 In re. **2** Nock. **3** NGA. **4** Sol.

42

Solutions

43

Across
1 Dais. 4 Ib. 5 Si. 6 Mojo.

Down
1 Diem. 2 AB. 3 Skio. 5 SJ.

44

Across
1 Balt. 5 Alia. 6 Baal. 7 Yerk.

Down
1 Baby. 2 Alae. 3 Liar. 4 Talk.

45

Across
1 Far. 4 Bona. 5 Ahoy. 6 Inn.

Down
1 Föhn. 2 Anon. 3 Ray. 4 BAI.

Solutions

Across
1 Isle. **5** Hum. **6** Tef. **7** Baff.

Down
2 Shea. **3** Luff. **4** Em. **6** TB.

46

Across
1 Vis. **4** Irid. **6** Mako. **7** QED.

Down
1 Vim. **2** Iraq. **3** Sike. **5** Dod.

47

Across
1 Gob. **4** Vina. **5** Ugly. **6** Gay.

Down
1 Giga-. **2** Only. **3** Bay. **4** Vug.

48

Solutions

49

Across
1 Iffy. 4 La. 5 Or. 6 Yoke.

Down
1 Illy. 2 FA. 3 Yare. 5 OK.

50

Across
1 Stop. 5 Taro. 6 Alar. 7 Yale.

Down
1 Stay. 2 Tala. 3 Oral. 4 Pore.

51

Across
1 Cos. 4 Shul. 5 Easy. 6 Art.

Down
1 Char. 2 Oust. 3 Sly. 4 Sea.

Solutions

Across
1 Skat. **5** Ado. **6** Uva. **7** Pawl.

Down
2 Kava. **3** Adaw. **4** To. **6** Up.

52

Across
1 Are. **4** Cong. **6** Tree. **7** Two.

Down
1 Act. **2** Rort. **3** Enew. **5** Geo-.

53

Across
1 Foe. **4** Gest. **5** Aria. **6** Mes.

Down
1 Fere. **2** -osis. **3** Eta. **4** Gam.

54

Solutions

55

Across
1 Nard. **4** Ob. **5** VE. **6** Gout.

Down
1 Nong. **2** AB. **3** Diet. **5** Vu.

56

Across
1 Atop. **5** Mali. **6** Phiz. **7** Sade.

Down
1 Amps. **2** Taha. **3** Olid. **4** Pize.

57

Across
1 Mog. **4** Fogy. **5** Atap. **6** REM.

Down
1 Mote. **2** Ogam. **3** Gyp. **4** Far.

Solutions

Across
1 Mohr. **5** Lev. **6** Ala. **7** Vade.

Down
2 Olla. **3** Head. **4** RV. **6** AV.

58

Across
1 Ule. **4** Rear. **6** Dash. **7** Neo.

Down
1 Urd. **2** Lean. **3** Ease. **5** Rho.

59

Across
1 Cru. **4** Vair. **5** Arvo. **6** Ute.

Down
1 Cart. **2** Rive. **3** Uro-. **4** Vau.

60

Solutions

61

Across
1 Soum. **4** In. **5** At. **6** Agio.

Down
1 Siva. **2** On. **3** Moto. **5** Ai.

62

Across
1 Tric. **5** Your. **6** Pura. **7** Open.

Down
1 Typo. **2** Roup. **3** Iure. **4** Cran.

63

Across
1 Hin. **4** Cine-. **5** Unto. **6** Ego.

Down
1 Hing. **2** Into. **3** Neo-. **4** Cue.

Solutions

Across
1 Oppo. **5** Lob. **6** Sou. **7** Fyrd.

Down
2 Ploy. **3** Pour. **4** Ob. **6** Sf.

64

Across
1 Fub. **4** Utah. **6** Dare. **7** Sew.

Down
1 Fud. **2** Utas. **3** Bare. **5** Hew.

65

Across
1 Ria. **4** Heft. **5** Orfe. **6** Bey.

Down
1 Rere. **2** Iffy. **3** Ate. **4** Hob.

66

Solutions

67

Across
1 Laic. **4** Os. **5** kW. **6** Fool.

Down
1 Loof. **2** As. **3** Cowl. **5** KO.

68

Across
1 Gabs. **5** Oboe. **6** Dyne. **7** Seal.

Down
1 Gods. **2** Abye. **3** Bona. **4** Seel.

69

Across
1 Wot. **4** Gaby. **5** Emir. **6** Let.

Down
1 Wame. **2** Obit. **3** Tyr. **4** Gel.

Solutions

Across
1 Scad. 5 Lsd. 6 Poi. 7 Tush.

Down
2 Clou. 3 As is. 4 DD. 6 PT.

70

Across
1 Lie. 4 Acts. 6 Mona. 7 Nay.

Down
1 Lam. 2 Icon. 3 Etna. 5 Say.

71

Across
1 Fro. 4 Pool. 5 Sild. 6 Ill.

Down
1 Foil. 2 Roll. 3 Old. 4 Psi.

72

Solutions

73

Across
1 Oort. 4 FX. 5 Is. 6 Yite.

Down
1 Ofay. 2 Ox. 3 Tose. 5 It.

74

Across
1 Spat. 5 Tace. 6 Airs. 7 Blot.

Down
1 Stab. 2 Pail. 3 Acro-. 4 Test.

75

Across
1 Fed. 4 Olla. 5 Cauk. 6 Awl.

Down
1 Flaw. 2 Elul. 3 Dak. 4 Oca.

Solutions

Across
1 Arba. **5** Eon. **6** Gid. **7** Oner.

Down
2 Rein. **3** Bode. **4** An. **6** Go.

76

Across
1 Bur. **4** Oral. **6** Ouzo. **7** Seg.

Down
1 Boo. **2** Urus. **3** Raze. **5** Log.

77

Across
1 Spa. **4** Skug. **5** Keta. **6** Apt.

Down
1 Skep. **2** Putt. **3** Aga. **4** Ska.

78

Solutions

79

Across
1 Kyle. **4** Re. **5** ER. **6** Buna.

Down
1 Krab. **2** Ye. **3** Eyra. **5** En.

80

Across
1 Tael. **5** Ogle. **6** Buba. **7** Yeah.

Down
1 Toby. **2** Ague. **3** Elba. **4** Leah.

81

Across
1 Mel. **4** Wage. **5** Agma. **6** Tea.

Down
1 Mage. **2** Egma. **3** Lea. **4** Wat.

Solutions

Across
1 Wang. **5** Coo. **6** She. **7** Hyle.

Down
2 Achy. **3** Noel. **4** Go. **6** Sh.

82

Across
1 Bap. **4** Unit. **6** Sech. **7** Way.

Down
1 Bus. **2** Anew. **3** Pica. **5** Thy.

83

Across
1 Ora. **4** Gris. **5** Etch. **6** -ese.

Down
1 Orts. **2** Rice. **3** Ash. **4** GEE.

84

Solutions

85

Across
1 Pink. **4** Ur-. **5** Is. **6** Loth.

Down
1 Purl. **2** IR. **3** Kish. **5** It.

86

Across
1 Marc. **5** Odea. **6** Kipp. **7** Otto.

Down
1 Moko. **2** Adit. **3** Rept. **4** Capo.

87

Across
1 Den. **4** Bice. **5** Reck. **6** Ate.

Down
1 Diet. **2** Ecce. **3** Nek. **4** Bra.

Solutions

Across
1 Fado. **5** Bok. **6** Ale. **7** Byke.

Down
2 Ably. **3** Doek. **4** OK. **6** Ab-.

88

Across
1 Wet. **4** Eric. **6** Bolo. **7** Sty.

Down
1 Web. **2** Eros. **3** Tilt. **5** Coy.

89

Across
1 Ban. **4** Some. **5** Help. **6** Era.

Down
1 Boer. **2** Amla. **3** Nep. **4** She.

90

Solutions

91

Across
1 Spam. **4** Ma. **5** RR. **6** Toil.

Down
1 Smit. **2** PA. **3** Marl. **5** RI.

92

Across
1 Kerb. **5** Idea. **6** Redd. **7** Knee.

Down
1 Kirk. **2** Eden. **3** Rede. **4** Bade.

93

Across
1 Kob. **4** Pele. **5** Espy. **6** The.

Down
1 Kesh. **2** Olpe. **3** Bey. **4** Pet.

Solutions

Across
1 Skag. **5** Ibo. **6** Aba. **7** Mesh.

Down
2 Kibe. **3** A bas. **4** Go. **6** AM.

Across
1 Kyu. **4** Ears. **6** Fust. **7** Day.

Down
1 Kef. **2** Yaud. **3** Ursa. **5** Sty.

Across
1 Hof. **4** Ease. **5** Lutz. **6** Olé.

Down
1 Haul. **2** Oste-. **3** Fez. **4** Elo.

Solutions

97

Across
1 Apso. **4** Gl. **5** QC. **6** Give.

Down
1 Agog. **2** Pi. **3** Once. **5** Qv.

98

Across
1 Seps. **5** Aqua. **6** Ruly. **7** Dies.

Down
1 Sard. **2** Equi-. **3** Pule. **4** Says.

99

Across
1 Hue. **4** Culm. **5** Aîné. **6** Baa.

Down
1 Huia. **2** Ulna. **3** Eme. **4** Cab.

Solutions

Across
1 Rigg. **5** Phi. **6** Hoe. **7** Idem.

Down
2 I-pod. **3** Ghee. **4** Gi. **6** Hi.

100

Across
1 Zoa. **4** Ebbs. **6** loll. **7** Ley.

Down
1 Zel. **2** Obol. **3** Able. **5** Sly.

101

Across
1 Tho'. **4** Oral. **5** Loke. **6** Dye.

Down
1 Troy. **2** Hake. **3** -ole. **4** Old.

102

Solutions

103

Across
1 Skol. **4** Eg. **5** lb. **6** Shoo.

Down
1 Sens. **2** Kg. **3** Lobo. **5** Lo.

104

Across
1 Sejm. **5** Area. **6** Gied. **7** Acre.

Down
1 Saga. **2** Eric. **3** Jeer. **4** Made.

105

Across
1 Arc. **4** Brio. **5** Ritz. **6** Ode.

Down
1 Arid. **2** Rite. **3** Coz. **4** Bro.

Solutions

Across
1 Jizz. **5** Too. **6** Sen. **7** Omen.

Down
2 Item. **3** Zone. **4** Zo. **6** So.

106

Across
1 Asp. **4** Swig. **6** Halo. **7** Neb.

Down
1 ASH. **2** Swan. **3** Pile. **5** Gob.

107

Across
1 Jat. **4** Puja. **5** Ajar. **6** Tux.

Down
1 Ju-ju. **2** Ajax. **3** Tar. **4** Pat.

108

Solutions

109

Across
1 Voar. **4** Io. **5** PG. **6** Twig.

Down
1 Vint. **2** Oo. **3** Ragg. **5** Pi.

110

Across
1 Pleb. **5** Aero. **6** Rand. **7** Trey.

Down
1 Part. **2** Lear. **3** Erne. **4** Body.

111

Across
1 Bin. **4** Safe. **5** Haff. **6** Ely.

Down
1 Baal. **2** Iffy. **3** Nef. **4** She.

Solutions

Across
1 Afro. **5** Oar. **6** Out. **7** Drub.

Down
2 Four. **3** Ratu. **4** Or. **6** OD.

112

Across
1 Imp. **4** Seer. **6** Mela. **7** Dad.

Down
1 Ism. **2** Meed. **3** Pela. **5** Rad.

113

Across
1 Boa. **4** Ainu. **5** Rack. **6** -ese.

Down
1 Bias. **2** Once. **3** Auk. **4** Are.

114

Solutions

115

Across
1 Flew. **4** Ra. **5** Do. **6** Yead.

Down
1 Fray. **2** LA. **3** Wood. **5** Da.

116

Across
1 Stem. **5** Paca. **6** Achy. **7** Rota.

Down
1 Spar. **2** Taco. **3** Echt. **4** Maya.

117

Across
1 Spy. **4** Hale. **5** Alit. **6** Tee.

Down
1 Sale. **2** Plié. **3** Yet. **4** Hat.

Solutions

Across
1 Abbé. **5** Old. **6** Ago. **7** Syce.

Down
2 Bogy. **3** Bloc. **4** Ed. **6** As.

118

Across
1 Poa. **4** Undo. **6** Suid. **7** STD.

Down
1 Pus. **2** Onus. **3** Adit. **5** Odd.

119

Across
1 Ana. **4** Slew. **5** Heal. **6** ESP.

Down
1 Ales. **2** Neap. **3** Awl. **4** She.

120

Solutions

121

Across
1 Eger. 4 Pu. 5 SA. 6 Amyl.

Down
1 Epha. 2 Gu. 3 Rial. 5 Sy-.

122

Across
1 Orfe. 5 Roar. 6 Rawn. 7 Anne.

Down
1 Orra. 2 Roan. 3 Fawn. 4 Erne.

123

Across
1 Red. 4 Ruru. 5 Iran. 6 Apt.

Down
1 Rurp. 2 Erat. 3 Dun. 4 Ria.

Solutions

Across
1 Sijo. 5 Rus. 6 Raj. 7 Aqua.

Down
2 Iraq. 3 Juju. 4 Os. 6 RA.

124

Across
1 Bay. 4 Utis. 6 Rape. 7 Psi.

Down
1 Bur. 2 Atap. 3 Yips. 5 Sei.

125

Across
1 Faw. 4 Pule. 5 Sned. 6 Ike.

Down
1 Funk. 2 Alee. 3 Wed. 4 Psi.

126

Solutions

127

Across
1 Spat. 4 Ex. 5 Ow. 6 Odds.

Down
1 Sego. 2 PX. 3 Taws. 5 Od.

128

Across
1 Sett. 5 Taha. 6 Oran. 7 Ante.

Down
1 Stoa. 2 Earn. 3 That. 4 Tane.

129

Across
1 Cas. 4 View. 5 Easy. 6 Toc.

Down
1 Ciao. 2 Aesc. 3 Swy. 4 Vet.

Solutions

Across
1 Raca. **5** Fey. **6** Han. **7** Erst.

Down
2 Afar. **3** Cens. **4** Ay. **6** He.

Across
1 Ebb. **4** Trio. **6** Huck. **7** Tee.

Down
1 Eth. **2** Brut. **3** Bice. **5** Oke.

Across
1 Dog. **4** Fane. **5** Idle. **6** Toy.

Down
1 Dado. **2** Only. **3** Gee. **4** Fit.

Solutions

133

Across
1 Airy. 4 Ff. 5 EW. 6 Yaps.

Down
1 Affy. 2 If. 3 Yaws. 5 EP.

134

Across
1 Apse. 5 Brat. 6 Loan. 7 Yama.

Down
1 Ably. 2 Proa. 3 Saam. 4 Etna.

135

Across
1 Two. 4 Rood. 5 Okra. 6 Ben.

Down
1 Toke. 2 Worn. 3 Oda. 4 Rob.

Solutions

Across
1 Bubo. **5** Nux. **6** Bin. **7** Etat.

Down
2 Unit. **3** Buna. **4** Ox. **6** Be.

136

Across
1 Egg. **4** Frab. **6** Tolu. **7** Gam.

Down
1 Eft. **2** Grog. **3** Gala. **5** Bum.

137

Across
1 Ada. **4** Shog. **5** Ooze. **6** Bye.

Down
1 Ahoy. **2** Doze. **3** Age. **4** Sob.

138

Solutions

139

Across
1 Opah. 4 Do. 5 My. 6 Stol.

Down
1 Odds. 2 Po. 3 Hwyl. 5 MO.

140

Across
1 Rant. 5 Urea. 6 Heck. 7 Rake.

Down
1 Ruhr. 2 Area. 3 Neck. 4 Take.

141

Across
1 Ate. 4 Tram. 5 Rube. 6 Ami.

Down
1 Arum. 2 Tabi. 3 EME. 4 Tra-.

Solutions

Across
1 Gale. 5 Mil. 6 Oak. 7 Thew.

Down
2 Amah. 3 Like. 4 El. 6 OT.

142

Across
1 Toe. 4 Upsy. 6 Nene. 7 New.

Down
1 Tun. 2 Open. 3 Esne. 5 Yew.

143

Across
1 Set. 4 Ante. 5 Goof. 6 Awn.

Down
1 Snow. 2 Eton. 3 Tef. 4 Aga.

144

Solutions

145

Across
1 Inly. **4** Fu. **5** El. **6** Yomp.

Down
1 Iffy. **2** Nu. **3** Yelp. **5** Em.

146

Across
1 Roti. **5** Over. **6** Tana. **7** Alee.

Down
1 Rota. **2** Oval. **3** Tene. **4** Irae.

147

Across
1 TCP. **4** Lure. **5** Yaud. **6** End.

Down
1 Tuan. **2** Crud. **3** Ped. **4** Lye.

Solutions

Across
1 Ambo. 5 Old. 6 Ore. 7 Robe.

Down
2 Moro. 3 Bleb. 4 Od. 6 OR.

Across
1 Boa. 4 lamb. 6 Stay. 7 She.

Down
1 Bis. 2 Oats. 3 Amah. 5 Bye.

Across
1 Lee. 4 Salk. 5 Esse. 6 Ate.

Down
1 Last. 2 Else. 3 Eke. 4 Sea.

Solutions

151

Across
1 Aitu. 4 zB. 5 In. 6 Nada.

Down
1 Azan. 2 Ib. 3 Ulna. 5 Id.

152

Across
1 Elat. 5 Ro-ro. 6 Skug. 7 Tems.

Down
1 Erst. 2 Loke. 3 Arum. 4 Togs.

153

Across
1 Moa. 4 Gimp. 5 Alit. 6 Tot.

Down
1 Milo. 2 Omit. 3 Apt. 4 Gat.

Solutions

Across
1 Unto. **5** Oik. **6** Eve. **7** Marl.

Down
2 Nova. **3** Tier. **4** OK. **6** Em.

Across
1 Dug. **4** Area. **6** Kell. **7** Ate.

Down
1 Dak. **2** Urea. **3** Gelt. **5** Ale.

Across
1 Eme. **4** Ever. **5** Gens. **6** Gnu.

Down
1 Even. **2** Menu. **3** Ers. **4** Egg.

Solutions

157

Across
1 Agio. 4 So. 5 Ut. 6 Yips.

Down
1 Ashy. 2 Go. 3 Oats. 5 Up.

158

Across
1 Brow. 5 Rave. 6 Agar. 7 Yale.

Down
1 Bray. 2 Raga. 3 Oval. 4 Were.

159

Across
1 Sec. 4 Typo. 5 Echo. 6 Lea.

Down
1 Syce. 2 Epha. 3 Coo. 4 Tel.

Solutions

Across
1 Mart. **5** Roe. **6** Ego. **7** Gods.

Down
2 Argo. **3** Rood. **4** Te. **6** eg.

160

Across
1 Goa. **4** Anno. **6** Muid. **7** SSA.

Down
1 Gam. **2** Onus. **3** Anis. **5** Oda.

161

Across
1 Sow. **4** Ziti. **5** Emit. **6** Lac.

Down
1 Sima. **2** Otic. **3** Wit. **4** Zel.

162

Solutions

163

Across
1 Egal. 4 Ko. 5 In. 6 Auto.

Down
1 Ekka. 2 Go. 3 Leno. 5 IT.

164

Across
1 Tose. 5 Wang. 6 Item. 7 Thea.

Down
1 Twit. 2 Oath. 3 Snee. 4 Egma.

165

Across
1 Leg. 4 Rima. 5 Amyl. 6 Gas.

Down
1 Lima. 2 Emys. 3 Gal. 4 Rag.

Solutions

Across
1 Raft. **5** Pro. **6** Gee. **7** Oxer.

Down
2 Apex. **3** Free. **4** To. **6** Go.

166

Across
1 Ask. **4** Lyon. **6** Anta. **7** Dob.

Down
1 A la. **2** Synd. **3** Koto. **5** Nab.

167

Across
1 Wet. **4** Char. **5** Eery. **6** End.

Down
1 When. **2** Eard. **3** Try. **4** Cee.

168

Solutions

169

Across
1 Eger. 4 So. 5 Up. 6 Yare.

Down
1 Espy. 2 Go. 3 Rape. 5 Ur-.

170

Across
1 Held. 5 Amir. 6 Rife. 7 Trey.

Down
1 Hart. 2 Emir. 3 Life. 4 Drey.

171

Across
1 Shy. 4 Epee. 5 Xema. 6 Ewe.

Down
1 Spew. 2 Heme. 3 Yea. 4 Exe.

Solutions

Across
1 Ankh. **5** Oer. **6** Ill. **7** Dopa.

Down
2 Nolo. **3** Kelp. **4** HR. **6** Id.

172

Across
1 Owl. **4** View. **6** Apse. **7** Een.

Down
1 Ova. **2** Wipe. **3** Lese. **5** Wen.

173

Across
1 Cru. **4** Leet. **5** Idle. **6** Dey.

Down
1 Cede. **2** Rely. **3** Ute. **4** Lid.

174

Solutions

175

Across
1 Bias. **4** On. **5** Go. **6** Axel.

Down
1 Bora. **2** In. **3** Skol. **5** Ge.

176

Across
1 Pray. **5** Lore. **6** Anil. **7** Teal.

Down
1 Plat. **2** Rone. **3** Aria. **4** Yell.

177

Across
1 Bel. **4** Lade. **5** Alga. **6** Dey.

Down
1 Bale. **2** Edgy. **3** Lea. **4** Lad.

Solutions

Across
1 Alma. **5** Ion. **6** Ask. **7** Skew.

Down
2 Lisk. **3** Moke. **4** An. **6** As.

178

Across
1 Lei. **4** Edda. **6** Kelt. **7** Nys.

Down
1 Lek. **2** Eden. **3** Idly. **5** Ats.

179

Across
1 Wag. **4** Dika. **5** Ares. **6** Gee.

Down
1 Wire. **2** Akee. **3** Gas. **4** Dag.

180

Solutions

181

Across
1 Culm. **4** It. **5** As. **6** Leno.

Down
1 Cill. **2** Ut. **3** Miso. **5** AN.

182

Across
1 Gear. **5** Elba. **6** Slut. **7** Teth.

Down
1 Gest. **2** Elle. **3** Abut. **4** Rath.

183

Across
1 Lea. **4** Herl. **5** Ease. **6** The.

Down
1 Leah. **2** Erse. **3** Ale. **4** Het.

Solutions

Across
1 Riss. **5** Dai. **6** Alt. **7** Oyer.

Down
2 Idly. **3** Sate. **4** Sl. **6** Ao.

184

Across
1 Hep. **4** Imam. **6** Pita. **7** Tet.

Down
1 Hip. **2** Emit. **3** Pate. **5** Mat.

185

Across
1 Spa. **4** Alar. **5** Souk. **6** Pea.

Down
1 Sloe. **2** Paua. **3** Ark. **4** Asp.

186

Solutions

187

Across
1 Bash. **4** Os. **5** Da. **6** Apex.

Down
1 Boma. **2** As. **3** Hoax. **5** De.

188

Across
1 Spas. **5** Iona. **6** Funk. **7** Tree.

Down
1 Sift. **2** Pour. **3** Anne. **4** Sake.

189

Across
1 Lap. **4** Sida. **5** Hazy. **6** Ere.

Down
1 Liar. **2** Adze. **3** Pay. **4** She.

Solutions

Across
1 Sung. **5** Roo. **6** Ado. **7** Suni.

Down
2 Urdu. **3** Noon. **4** Go. **6** As.

190

Across
1 AKA. **4** Silk. **6** Sloe. **7** Led.

Down
1 Ass. **2** Kill. **3** Aloe. **5** Ked.

191

Across
1 Tic. **4** Dodo. **5** Ably. **6** Lye.

Down
1 Toby. **2** Idle. **3** Coy. **4** Dal.

192

Solutions

193

Across
1 Vang. 4 Ob. 5 Or. 6 Rife.

Down
1 Voar. 2 AB. 3 Gyre. 5 Of.

194

Across
1 Sist. 5 Arty. 6 Goor. 7 Ante.

Down
1 Saga. 2 Iron. 3 Stot. 4 Tyre.

195

Across
1 Ago. 4 Snit. 5 Port. 6 And.

Down
1 Anon. 2 Gird. 3 OTT. 4 Spa.

Solutions

Across
1 Scab. **5** Ule. **6** Elf. **7** Oman.

Down
2 Culm. **3** Alfa. **4** Be. **6** EO.

196

Across
1 End. **4** Lour. **6** Koka. **7** Ket.

Down
1 Elk. **2** Nook. **3** Duke. **5** Rat.

197

Across
1 Lap. **4** Lipa. **5** Aran. **6** Way.

Down
1 Lira. **2** Apay. **3** Pan. **4** Law.

198

Solutions

199

Across
1 Chou. 4 Lo. 5 Be. 6 Proa.

Down
1 Clop. 2 Ho. 3 Uvea. 5 Bo.

200

Across
1 Stag. 5 Oily. 6 Clam. 7 Keep.

Down
1 Sock. 2 Tile. 3 Alae. 4 Gymp.

201

Across
1 Bad. 4 Toco. 5 Oath. 6 Era.

Down
1 Boar. 2 Acta. 3 Doh. 4 Toe.

Solutions

Across
1 Able. 5 Rap. 6 Air. 7 Moko.

Down
2 Brio. 3 Lark. 4 EP. 6 AM.

202

Across
1 Amp. 4 Rale. 6 Myal. 7 Any.

Down
1 Arm. 2 Maya. 3 Plan. 5 Ely.

203

Across
1 Ask. 4 Ague. 5 Gory. 6 One.

Down
1 Agon. 2 Sure. 3 Key. 4 Ago.

204

Solutions

205

Across
1 Palp. **4** Oy. **5** Wu. **6** Leet.

Down
1 Poll. **2** Ay. **3** Pout. **5** We.

206

Across
1 Slow. **5** Mosh. **6** Esse. **7** What.

Down
1 Smew. **2** Losh. **3** Ossa. **4** Whet.

207

Across
1 Bye. **4** Mull. **5** Abet. **6** GOM.

Down
1 Bubo. **2** Ylem. **3** ELT. **4** Mag.

Solutions

Across
1 Scam. **5** Olé. **6** Goa. **7** Oppo.

Down
2 Coop. **3** Alap. **4** ME. **6** Go.

208

Across
1 Ora. **4** Lorn. **6** Mino. **7** Lag.

Down
1 Olm. **2** Roil. **3** Arna. **5** Nog.

209

Across
1 Poa. **4** Samp. **5** Alit. **6** Nit.

Down
1 Pali. **2** Omit. **3** Apt. **4** San.

210

Solutions

211

Across
1 Cusp. 4 OP. 5 Do. 6 Bevy.

Down
1 Comb. 2 Up. 3 Ploy. 5 DV.

212

Across
1 Up to. 5 Dial. 6 Arid. 7 Lily.

Down
1 Udal. 2 Piri-. 3 Tail. 4 Oldy.

213

Across
1 Boa. 4 Taig. 5 Erne. 6 Dak.

Down
1 Bara. 2 Oink. 3 Age. 4 Ted.

Solutions

Across
1 Plap. **5** Ubi. **6** Oca. **7** Neck.

Down
2 Luce. **3** Abac. **4** Pi. **6** On.

214

Across
1 Cap. **4** Odic. **6** Bapu. **7** REM.

Down
1 Cob. **2** Adar. **3** Pipe. **5** Cum.

215

Across
1 Die. **4** Phot. **5** Rota. **6** E-la.

Down
1 Dhol. **2** Iota. **3** Eta. **4** Pre-.

216

Solutions

217

Across
1 Pith. **4** At. **5** FL. **6** Leet.

Down
1 Pawl. **2** It. **3** Holt. **5** Fé.

218

Across
1 Acta. **5** Clem. **6** Heli. **7** Egad.

Down
1 Ache. **2** Cleg. **3** Tela. **4** Amid.

219

Across
1 Nos. **4** Mela. **5** Eric. **6** Udo.

Down
1 Nerd. **2** Olio. **3** Sac. **4** Meu.

Solutions

Across
1 Plié. 5 Ion. 6 Set. 7 Onan.

Down
2 Lien. 3 Iota. 4 En. 6 So.

220

Across
1 Poa. 4 Orzo. 6 Scar. 7 Ant.

Down
1 Pos. 2 Orca. 3 Azan. 5 Ort.

221

Across
1 Eme. 4 Oval. 5 Pott. 6 Tee.

Down
1 Evoe. 2 Mate. 3 ELT. 4 Opt.

222

Solutions

223

Across
1 Atok. 4 Jo. 5 At. 6 Xema.

Down
1 Ajax. 2 To. 3 Kata. 5 AM.

224

Across
1 Slaw. 5 Kava. 6 User. 7 Germ.

Down
1 Skug. 2 Lase. 3 Aver. 4 Warm.

225

Across
1 Zuz. 4 Pule. 5 Open. 6 Tax.

Down
1 Zupa. 2 Ulex. 3 Zen. 4 Pot.

Solutions

Across
1 Shad. 5 Ido. 6 Ski. 7 Sett.

Down
2 Hike. 3 Adit. 4 Do. 6 SS.

226

Across
1 Eke. 4 Love. 6 Khor. 7 Leg.

Down
1 Elk. 2 Kohl. 3 Evoe. 5 Erg.

227

Across
1 Sky. 4 Chai. 5 Iron. 6 DIN.

Down
1 Shri. 2 Kaon. 3 Yin. 4 Cid.

228

Solutions

229

Across
1 Odds. 4 Ae. 5 Ti. 6 Huer.

Down
1 Oath. 2 De. 3 Shir. 5 Te.

230

Across
1 Smog. 5 Eoan. 6 Rusa. 7 Fett.

Down
1 Serf. 2 Moue. 3 Oast. 4 Gnat.

231

Across
1 May. 4 Core. 5 Ohms. 6 Try.

Down
1 Mohr. 2 Army. 3 Yes. 4 Cot.

Solutions

Across
1 Ipse. **5** Lax. **6** Pam. **7** Typo.

Down
2 Play. **3** Samp. **4** Ex. **6** PT.

232

Across
1 Viz. **4** Ebon. **6** Tire. **7** Dip.

Down
1 Vet. **2** Ibid. **3** Zori. **5** Nep.

233

Across
1 Bra. **4** Foal. **5** Else. **6** Eth.

Down
1 Bolt. **2** Rash. **3** Ale. **4** Fee.

234

Solutions

235

Across
1 Ages. 4 Ho. 5 IR. 6 Yoof.

Down
1 Ahoy. 2 Go. 3 Serf. 5 Io.

236

Across
1 Deus. 5 Urge. 6 Moll. 7 As if.

Down
1 Duma. 2 Eros. 3 Ugli. 4 Self.

237

Across
1 Spa. 4 Poon. 5 Iona. 6 Any.

Down
1 Soon. 2 Pony. 3 Ana. 4 Pia.

Solutions

Across
1 Ecru. **5** Het. **6** Mas. **7** Otto.

Down
2 Chat. **3** Rest. **4** Ut. **6** Mo.

238

Across
1 Ska. **4** Worm. **6** Yoga. **7** Kob.

Down
1 Swy. **2** Kook. **3** Argo. **5** Mab.

239

Across
1 Nos. **4** Barf. **5** Tizz. **6** UFO.

Down
1 Naif. **2** Orzo. **3** Sfz. **4** BTU.

240

Solutions

241

Across
1 Tomb. **4** Up. **5** Gi. **6** Pout.

Down
1 Tump. **2** Op. **3** Bait. **5** Gu.

242

Across
1 Saga. **5** Onyx. **6** Fore. **7** Tael.

Down
1 Soft. **2** Anoa. **3** Gyre. **4** Axel.

243

Across
1 Cro. **4** Faex. **5** Espy. **6** Zap.

Down
1 Casa. **2** Repp. **3** Oxy-. **4** Fez.

Solutions

Across
1 Up to. **5** Oar. **6** Ion. **7** Frap.

Down
2 Poor. **3** Tana. **4** Or. **6** If.

244

Across
1 Née. **4** Oats. **6** Grue. **7** Lit.

Down
1 Nog. **2** Earl. **3** Etui. **5** Set.

245

Across
1 Bow. **4** Purr. **5** Affy. **6** Doe.

Down
1 Bufo. **2** Orfe. **3** Wry. **4** Pad.

246

Solutions

247

Across
1 Op-ed. 4 Ru. 5 Ai. 6 Xyst.

Down
1 Oryx. 2 Pu. 3 Doit. 5 As.

248

Across
1 Ruff. 5 Inia. 6 Find. 7 Foes.

Down
1 Riff. 2 Unio. 3 Fine. 4 Fads.

249

Across
1 Mew. 4 Coda. 5 Alit. 6 Bet.

Down
1 Mole. 2 Edit. 3 Wat. 4 Cab.

Solutions

Across
1 Oman. **5** Ecu. **6** Ute. **7** Pern.

Down
2 Mete. **3** Acer. **4** Nu. **6** Up.

250

Across
1 Bat. **4** Oboe. **6** Kelt. **7** Tea.

Down
1 Bok. **2** Abet. **3** Tole. **5** Eta.

251

Across
1 Art. **4** Stoa. **5** Pout. **6** Apt.

Down
1 Atop. **2** Rout. **3** Tat. **4** Spa.

252

Solutions

253

Across
1 Oner. 4 My. 5 Is. 6 Ulna.

Down
1 Ombu. 2 NY. 3 Rusa. 5 In.

254

Across
1 Berg. 5 Over. 6 Mese. 7 Arty.

Down
1 Boma. 2 Ever. 3 Rest. 4 Grey.

255

Across
1 Sea. 4 Chap. 5 Oust. 6 Sty.

Down
1 Shut. 2 Easy. 3 Apt. 4 Cos.

Solutions

Across
1 Edge. **5** Eon. **6** Inn. **7** Fegs.

Down
2 Dene. **3** Gong. **4** En. **6** If.

256

Across
1 Tod. **4** Upon. **6** Pene. **7** Nab.

Down
1 Tup. **2** Open. **3** Dona. **5** Neb.

257

Across
1 Lag. **4** Pika. **5** Iris. **6** Tan.

Down
1 Lira. **2** Akin. **3** Gas. **4** Pit.

258

Solutions

259

Across
1 Koph. 4 ER. 5 PR. 6 Tige.

Down
1 Kent. 2 Or. 3 Hare. 5 PG.

260

Across
1 Pass. 5 Lilo. 6 Udon. 7 Gate.

Down
1 Plug. 2 Aida. 3 Slot. 4 Sone.

261

Across
1 Bug. 4 Mana. 5 Obit. 6 Get.

Down
1 Babe. 2 Unit. 3 Gat. 4 Mog.

Solutions

Across
1 Smit. **5** Ora. **6** Elo. **7** Tang.

Down
2 Mola. **3** Iron. **4** Ta. **6** Et.

262

Across
1 Tot. **4** Abet. **6** Moxa. **7** ETD.

Down
1 Tam. **2** Oboe. **3** Text. **5** Tad.

263

Across
1 Boa. **4** Lanx. **5** Able. **6** May.

Down
1 Baba. **2** Only. **3** Axe. **4** Lam.

264

Solutions

265

Across
1 Gash. **4** It. **5** By. **6** Proa.

Down
1 Gimp. **2** At. **3** Hoya. **5** BO.

266

Across
1 Goss. **5** Olea. **6** Blag. **7** Yale.

Down
1 Goby. **2** Olla. **3** Seal. **4** Sage.

267

Across
1 Ess. **4** Oupa. **5** Frit. **6** Fon.

Down
1 Euro. **2** Spin. **3** Sat. **4** Off.

Solutions

Across
1 Lore. **5** Nix. **6** All. **7** Hyla.

Down
2 Only. **3** Rill. **4** Ex. **6** Ah.

268

Across
1 Ubi. **4** Gare. **6** Haik. **7** LSE.

Down
1 Ugh. **2** Baal. **3** Iris. **5** Eke.

269

Across
1 Bar. **4** Fane. **5** Lunt. **6** Udo.

Down
1 Baud. **2** Anno. **3** Ret. **4** Flu.

270

Solutions

271

Across
1 Achy. 4 Da. 5 OR. 6 Esse.

Down
1 Adze. 2 Ca. 3 Yore. 5 Os.

272

Across
1 Geta. 5 Aval. 6 Fink. 7 Flay.

Down
1 Gaff. 2 Evil. 3 Tana. 4 Alky.

273

Across
1 Maa. 4 Fisc. 5 Edit. 6 Dis.

Down
1 Midi. 2 As is. 3 Act. 4 Fed.

Solutions

Across
1 Gobo. **5** Nux. **6** Her. **7** Errs.

Down
2 Oner. **3** Burr. **4** Ox. **6** He.

274

Across
1 Ago. **4** Loge. **6** Purl. **7** Tet.

Down
1 Alp. **2** Gout. **3** Ogre. **5** Elt.

275

Across
1 Soc. **4** Opah. **5** Vase. **6** Art.

Down
1 Spar. **2** Oast. **3** Che. **4** Ova.

276

Solutions

277

Across
1 Tola. 4 If. 5 AV. 6 Into.

Down
1 Tiki. 2 Of. 3 Arvo. 5 At.

278

Across
1 Burr. 5 Arie. 6 Nave. 7 Clef.

Down
1 Banc. 2 Ural. 3 Rive. 4 Reef.

279

Across
1 Coo. 4 Chad. 5 Rase. 6 Opt.

Down
1 Chap. 2 Oast. 3 Ode. 4 Cro.

Solutions

Across
1 Asti. **5** Tit. **6** Ken. **7** Open.

Down
2 Step. **3** Tine. **4** It. **6** KO.

280

Across
1 Ilk. **4** Dais. **6** Ombu. **7** Ben.

Down
1 Ido. **2** Lamb. **3** Kibe. **5** Sun.

281

Across
1 Ash. **4** Plea. **5** Lees. **6** Yen.

Down
1 Alee. **2** Seen. **3** Has. **4** Ply.

282

Solutions

283

Across
1 Adze. 4 To. 5 Or. 6 Coda.

Down
1 Atoc. 2 Do. 3 Ezra. 5 OD.

284

Across
1 Topi. 5 Oban. 6 Nock. 7 Gley.

Down
1 Tong. 2 Obol. 3 Pace. 4 Inky.

285

Across
1 Dop. 4 Pupa. 5 Repp. 6 Elo.

Down
1 Duel. 2 Oppo. 3 Pap. 4 Pre-.

Solutions

Across
1 Tron. **5** One. **6** Ave. **7** Sere.

Down
2 Rove. **3** Oner. **4** Ne. **6** As.

286

Across
1 Cam. **4** Oxon. **6** Lino. **7** Saw.

Down
1 Col. **2** Axis. **3** Mona. **5** Now.

287

Across
1 Tee. **4** Mong. **5** Agog. **6** Taw.

Down
1 Toga. **2** Enow. **3** Egg. **4** Mat.

288

Solutions

289

Across
1 Mohs. 4 In. 5 AG. 6 Arno.

Down
1 Mica. 2 On. 3 Sago. 5 An.

290

Across
1 Graf. 5 Aide. 6 Stoa. 7 Pest.

Down
1 Gasp. 2 Rite. 3 Ados. 4 Feat.

291

Across
1 Ska. 4 Ahoy. 5 Yale. 6 Rho.

Down
1 Shah. 2 Kolo. 3 Aye. 4 Ayr.

Solutions

Across
1 Gamb. **5** Loy. **6** Elo. **7** Myth.

Down
2 Ally. **3** Moot. **4** By. **6** Em.

292

Across
1 Ecu. **4** Song. **6** Sida. **7** Feu.

Down
1 -ess. **2** Coif. **3** Unde. **5** Gau.

293

Across
1 Icy. **4** Sole. **5** Onan. **6** Gam.

Down
1 Iona. **2** Clam. **3** Yen. **4** Sog.

294

Solutions

295

Across
1 Aged. 4 No. 5 sf. 6 Hoot.

Down
1 Ankh. 2 Go. 3 Deft. 5 So.

296

Across
1 Blae. 5 Oont. 6 Muon. 7 Anna.

Down
1 Boma. 2 Loun. 3 Anon. 4 Etna.

297

Across
1 Hap. 4 Sept. 5 Area. 6 Cox.

Down
1 Hero. 2 Apex. 3 Pta. 4 Sac.

Solutions

Across
1 Shaw. **5** Ule. **6** Ago. **7** Sook.

Down
2 Hugo. **3** Aloo. **4** We. **6** As.

298

Across
1 Are. **4** Yegg. **6** Edge. **7** Dye.

Down
1 Aye. **2** Redd. **3** Eggy. **5** Gee.

299

Across
1 Sky. **4** Sloe. **5** Holt. **6** Ego.

Down
1 Slog. **2** Kolo. **3** Yet. **4** She.

300

Solutions

301

Across
1 Agog. 4 Jo. 5 Om. 6 Risp.

Down
1 Ajar. 2 Go. 3 Gimp. 5 Os.

302

Across
1 Lant. 5 Aloe. 6 Glum. 7 Sans.

Down
1 Lags. 2 Alla. 3 Noun. 4 Tems.

303

Across
1 Aka. 4 Bent. 5 Eros. 6 Yob.

Down
1 Aero. 2 Knob. 3 ATS. 4 Bey.

Solutions

Across
1 Deft. **5** Ala. **6** Ace. **7** Shea.

Down
2 Each. **3** Flee. **4** TA. **6** As.

304

Across
1 Bis. **4** Ecad. **6** Loke. **7** Neb.

Down
1 Bel. **2** Icon. **3** Sake. **5** Deb.

305

Across
1 Lew. **4** Tope. **5** Akin. **6** Tic.

Down
1 Loki. **2** Epic. **3** Wen. **4** Tat.

306

Solutions

307

Across
1 OMOV. 4 Fa. 5 Oi. 6 Yawl.

Down
1 Ofay. 2 Ma. 3 Vail. 5 Ow.

308

Across
1 Pass. 5 Ouma. 6 Slug. 7 Taro.

Down
1 Post. 2 Aula. 3 Smur. 4 Sago.

309

Across
1 Osp. 4 Ague. 5 Flic. 6 Ted.

Down
1 Ogle. 2 Suid. 3 Pec. 4 Aft.

Solutions

Across
1 Asci. **5** Tat. **6** Oar. **7** Rype.

Down
2 Stay. **3** Carp. **4** It. **6** OR.

310

Across
1 Pod. **4** Alit. **6** Miso. **7** Dso.

Down
1 Pam. **2** Olid. **3** Diss. **5** Too.

311

Across
1 Apt. **4** Pila. **5** Enow. **6** Get.

Down
1 Aîné. **2** Plot. **3** Taw. **4** Peg.

312

Solutions

313

Across
1 Abut. **4** QC. **5** Of. **6** Ainu.

Down
1 Aqua. **2** BC. **3** Tofu. **5** On.

314

Across
1 Ship. **5** Poor. **6** Anta. **7** Team.

Down
1 Spat. **2** Hone. **3** Iota. **4** Pram.

315

Across
1 LED. **4** Midi. **5** Ergs. **6** Tay.

Down
1 Lira. **2** Edgy. **3** Dis. **4** Met.

Solutions

Across
1 Urdu. 5 Out. 6 Ute. 7 Pelf.

Down
2 Rote. 3 Duel. 4 Ut. 6 Up.

316

Across
1 Ice. 4 Shim. 6 Mare. 7 Pew.

Down
1 Ism. 2 Chap. 3 Eire. 5 Mew.

317

Across
1 Pet. 4 Lava. 5 Anon. 6 Gee.

Down
1 Pane. 2 Evoe. 3 Tan. 4 Lag.

318

Solutions

319

Across
1 Anil. **4** Go. **5** DV. **6** Orgy.

Down
1 Agio. **2** No. **3** Levy. **5** DG.

320

Across
1 Doll. **5** Aria. **6** Flew. **7** Tenn.

Down
1 Daft. **2** Orle. **3** Lien. **4** Lawn.

321

Across
1 Hop. **4** Haka. **5** Errs. **6** Pea.

Down
1 Hare. **2** Okra. **3** Pas. **4** Hep.

Solutions

Across
1 Glib. **5** Ide. **6** Udo. **7** Mola.

Down
2 Lido. **3** Idol. **4** Be. **6** Um.

322

Across
1 Doe. **4** Able. **6** Kell. **7** Yam.

Down
1 Dak. **2** Obey. **3** Ella. **5** Elm.

323

Across
1 Tee. **4** Oral. **5** Rest. **6** Fey.

Down
1 Tree. **2** Easy. **3** ELT. **4** Orf.

324

Solutions

325

Across
1 Adry. 4 To. 5 Em. 6 Kelp.

Down
1 Atok. 2 Do. 3 Yomp. 5 El.

326

Across
1 Chad. 5 Lava. 6 Alec. 7 Yore.

Down
1 Clay. 2 Halo. 3 Aver. 4 Dace.

327

Across
1 Dae. 4 Pell. 5 Omit. 6 Dot.

Down
1 Demo. 2 Alit. 3 ELT. 4 Pod.

Solutions

Across
1 Iffy. **5** Lee. **6** Mas. **7** Unto.

Down
2 Flan. **3** Fest. **4** Ye. **6** Mu.

328

Across
1 Duo. **4** Ingo. **6** Pied. **7** Ted.

Down
1 Dip. **2** Unit. **3** Ogee. **5** Odd.

329

Across
1 Nap. **4** Saga. **5** Oval. **6** Per.

Down
1 Nave. **2** Agar. **3** PAL. **4** Sop.

330

Solutions

331

Across
1 Ammo. 4 Bo. 5 So. 6 Limn.

Down
1 Abel. 2 Mo. 3 Oxon. 5 SM.

332

Across
1 Toad. 5 Ably. 6 Souk. 7 Semé.

Down
1 Tass. 2 Oboe. 3 Alum. 4 Dyke.

333

Across
1 Tom. 4 Cute. 5 Obit. 6 Sac.

Down
1 Tuba. 2 Otic. 3 Met. 4 Cos.

Solutions

Across
1 Stum. **5** Ago. **6** Til. **7** Olio.

Down
2 Tail. **3** Ugli. **4** MO. **6** To.

334

Across
1 Mot. **4** Ilea. **6** Ling. **7** Dee.

Down
1 Mil. **2** Olid. **3** Tene. **5** Age.

335

Across
1 Bis. **4** Loth. **5** Smee. **6** Dam.

Down
1 Boma. **2** Item. **3** She. **4** LSD.

336

Solutions

337

Across
1 Arab. 4 Ka. 5 TB. 6 EFTA.

Down
1 Akee. 2 Ra. 3 Baba. 5 TT.

338

Across
1 Fame. 5 Unit. 6 Nana. 7 Knit.

Down
1 Funk. 2 Anan. 3 Mini. 4 Etat.

339

Across
1 Bot. 4 Mome. 5 Olea. 6 Tor.

Down
1 Bolo. 2 Omer. 3 Tea. 4 Mot.

Solutions

Across
1 Efts. **5** Rum. **6** Pam. **7** Tupi.

Down
2 Frau. **3** Tump. **4** SM. **6** PT.

340

Across
1 Elt. **4** Loop. **6** Motu. **7** Ket.

Down
1 Elm. **2** Look. **3** Tote. **5** Put.

341

Across
1 Tib. **4** Kara. **5** Icon. **6** Ten.

Down
1 Tace. **2** Iron. **3** Ban. **4** Kit.

342

Solutions

343

Across
1 Stot. **4** Po. **5** Da. **6** Kook.

Down
1 Spek. **2** To. **3** Teak. **5** Do.

344

Across
1 Ross. **5** Opah. **6** Kuna. **7** Esky.

Down
1 Roke. **2** Opus. **3** Sank. **4** Shay.

345

Across
1 K'ri. **4** Lair. **5** Smee. **6** Dam.

Down
1 Kama. **2** Riem. **3** Ire. **4** LSD.

Solutions

Across
1 Rigg. **5** Rho. **6** Hoe. **7** Anew.

Down
2 Iron. **3** Ghee. **4** Go. **6** Ha.

346

Across
1 Asp. **4** Suid. **6** Seer. **7** Try.

Down
1 Ass. **2** Suet. **3** Pier. **5** Dry.

347

Across
1 Dom. **4** Pula. **5** Epic. **6** Ted.

Down
1 Dupe. **2** Olid. **3** Mac. **4** Pet.

348

Solutions

349

Across
1 Jura. 4 Et. 5 Ae. 6 Fess.

Down
1 Jeff. 2 Ut. 3 Ages. 5 As.

350

Across
1 Otto. 5 Areg. 6 Rale. 7 Span.

Down
1 Oars. 2 Trap. 3 Tela. 4 Ogen.

351

Across
1 Tee. 4 Tilt. 5 Amah. 6 Gen.

Down
1 Time. 2 Elan. 3 Eth. 4 Tag.

Solutions

Across
1 Alga. **5** Alt. **6** Ido. **7** Typo.

Down
2 Lady. **3** Glop. **4** At. **6** It.

Across
1 Raj. **4** Iron. **6** Meso-. **7** Shy.

Down
1 Rim. **2** Ares. **3** Josh. **5** Noy.

Across
1 Asp. **4** Oche. **5** Prog. **6** Ted.

Down
1 Acre. **2** Shod. **3** Peg. **4** Opt.

Solutions

Solutions

Across
1 Ecco. **5** Hen. **6** Oud. **7** Stew.

Down
2 Chut. **3** Cede. **4** On. **6** Os.

Across
1 Hie. **4** Acta. **6** Gout. **7** Nie.

Down
1 Hag. **2** Icon. **3** Etui. **5** Ate.

Across
1 Ass. **4** Ammo. **5** Ebon. **6** Sog.

Down
1 Ambo. **2** Smog. **3** Son. **4** Aes.

Solutions

361

Across
1 Half. **4** It. **5** Mu. **6** Styx.

Down
1 Hiss. **2** At. **3** Flux. **5** My.

362

Across
1 Scan. **5** Arco. **6** Kami. **7** Ewer.

Down
1 Sake. **2** Craw. **3** Acme. **4** Noir.

363

Across
1 Fra. **4** Doab. **5** Espy. **6** Est.

Down
1 Foss. **2** Rapt. **3** Aby. **4** Dee.

Solutions

Across
1 Garb. **5** Fey. **6** Oft. **7** Dyer.

Down
2 Affy. **3** Rete. **4** By. **6** Od.

364

Across
1 CAT. **4** Echo. **6** Phat. **7** ENT.

Down
1 Cep. **2** Ache. **3** Than. **5** OTT.

365

Across
1 Are. **4** Plat. **5** Ossa. **6** Top.

Down
1 Also. **2** Rasp. **3** ETA. **4** Pot.

366

Solutions

367

Across
1 Limb. 4 On. 5 It. 6 Knot.

Down
1 Look. 2 In. 3 Butt. 5 Io.

368

Across
1 Tael. 5 Ugly. 6 Cist. 7 Knee.

Down
1 Tuck. 2 Agin. 3 Else. 4 Lyte.

369

Across
1 Bag. 4 Cire. 5 Haul. 6 Ism.

Down
1 Bias. 2 Arum. 3 Gel. 4 Chi.

Solutions

Across
1 Grot. 5 Ego. 6 Oda. 7 Mome.

Down
2 Redo. 3 Ogam. 4 To. 6 Om.

370

Across
1 Fob. 4 Ibis. 6 Tole. 7 Eke.

Down
1 Fit. 2 Oboe. 3 Bilk. 5 See.

371

Across
1 Mea. 4 Perk. 5 Ossa. 6 Tee.

Down
1 Mese. 2 Erse. 3 AKA. 4 Pot.

372

Solutions

373

Across
1 Abbe. 4 De. 5 In. 6 Ease.

Down
1 Adze. 2 Be. 3 Erne. 5 IS.

374

Across
1 Rahu. 5 Ares. 6 File. 7 Tems.

Down
1 Raft. 2 Arie. 3 Helm. 4 Uses.

375

Across
1 Pam. 4 Gala. 5 Icon. 6 Née.

Down
1 Pace. 2 Aloe. 3 Man. 4 Gin.

Solutions

Across
1 Mara. **5** Van. **6** Ben. **7** Asar.

Down
2 Aves. **3** Rana. **4** An. **6** Ba.

376

Across
1 Ers. **4** Balk. **6** Brie. **7** Apt.

Down
1 Ebb. **2** Ra-ra. **3** Slip. **5** Ket.

377

Across
1 Rat. **4** Rape. **5** Ossa. **6** Tee.

Down
1 Rase. **2** Apse. **3** Tea. **4** Rot.

378

Solutions

379

Across
1 Jiff. **4** Os. **5** Bo. **6** Heel.

Down
1 Josh. **2** Is. **3** Fool. **5** Be.

380

Across
1 Late. **5** Aval. **6** Moxa. **7** Anan.

Down
1 Lama. **2** Avon. **3** Taxa. **4** Elan.

381

Across
1 Opp. **4** Chay. **5** Onyx. **6** Yes.

Down
1 Ohne. **2** Pays. **3** Pyx. **4** Coy.

Solutions

Across
1 Otto. **5** Wap. **6** Sen. **7** Fegs.

Down
2 Twee. **3** Tang. **4** Op. **6** Sf.

382

Across
1 Use. **4** Blab. **6** Iota. **7** ESP.

Down
1 Ubi. **2** Sloe. **3** Eats. **5** Bap.

383

Across
1 Sap. **4** Loma. **5** Aril. **6** Cad.

Down
1 Sora. **2** Amid. **3** PAL. **4** Lac.

384

Solutions

385

Across
1 Skat. **4** HA. **5** SA. **6** Amok.

Down
1 Shia. **2** Ka. **3** Teak. **5** So.

386

Across
1 Eels. **5** Spee. **6** Shar. **7** Ease.

Down
1 Esse. **2** Epha. **3** Leas. **4** Sere.

387

Across
1 MBE. **4** Leir. **5** Ages. **6** Gar.

Down
1 Mega. **2** Bier. **3** Ers. **4** Lag.

Solutions

Across
1 Maya. **5** Lid. **6** Pit. **7** Item.

Down
2 Alit. **3** Yite. **4** AD. **6** Pi.

388

Across
1 Goa. **4** Ombu. **6** Baud. **7** NTS.

Down
1 Gob. **2** Oman. **3** Abut. **5** Uds.

389

Across
1 Off. **4** Ogle. **5** Trez. **6** Tew.

Down
1 Ogre. **2** Flew. **3** Fez. **4** OTT.

390

Solutions

391

Across
1 Gilt. 4 At. 5 On. 6 Yama.

Down
1 Gamy. 2 It. 3 Tana. 5 OM.

392

Across
1 Pelf. 5 Etui. 6 Tara. 7 Stet.

Down
1 Pets. 2 Etat. 3 Lure. 4 Fiat.

393

Across
1 LRP. 4 Jiao. 5 Urge. 6 Dag.

Down
1 Lira. 2 Ragg. 3 Poe. 4 Jud.

Solutions

Across
1 Fard. **5** Ria. **6** Ebb. **7** Mash.

Down
2 Arba. **3** Ribs. **4** Da. **6** Em.

394

Across
1 Mac. **4** Idle. **6** Riel. **7** Two.

Down
1 Mir. **2** Adit. **3** Clew. **5** Elo.

395

Across
1 Ska. **4** Goop. **5** Hint. **6** Ilk.

Down
1 Soil. **2** Konk. **3** Apt. **4** Ghi.

396

Solutions

397

Across
1 Moth. 4 In. 5 pH. 6 Aria.

Down
1 Mica. 2 On. 3 Ha-ha. 5 Pl.

398

Across
1 Cred. 5 Ooze. 6 Mora. 7 Adar.

Down
1 Coma. 2 Rood. 3 Ezra. 4 Dear.

399

Across
1 Law. 4 Hila. 5 Unit. 6 Get.

Down
1 Line. 2 Alit. 3 Wat. 4 Hug.

Solutions

Across
1 Dhol. **5** Ora. **6** Uva. **7** Pelf.

Down
2 Hove. **3** Oral. **4** La. **6** Up.

400

Daily Mail

Also available from Hamlyn...
Daily Mail New Cryptic Crosswords – £5.99

Volume 1: 978-0-600-61635-1
Volume 2: 978-0-600-61640-5
Volume 3: 978-0-600-61709-9
Volume 4: 978-0-600-61812-6
Volume 5: 978-0-600-61845-4
Volume 6: 978-0-600-61878-2
Volume 7: 978-0-600-61970-3
Volume 8: 978-0-600-61971-0
Volume 9: 978-0-600-61979-6
Volume 10: 978-0-600-62102-7
Volume 11: 978-0-600-62103-4
Volume 12: 978-0-600-62124-9

To order these or other *Daily Mail* puzzle books visit
www.maillife.co.uk/books or call 0845 155 0720